The Boy Who Rode The Dragon

by
Ian Feldman

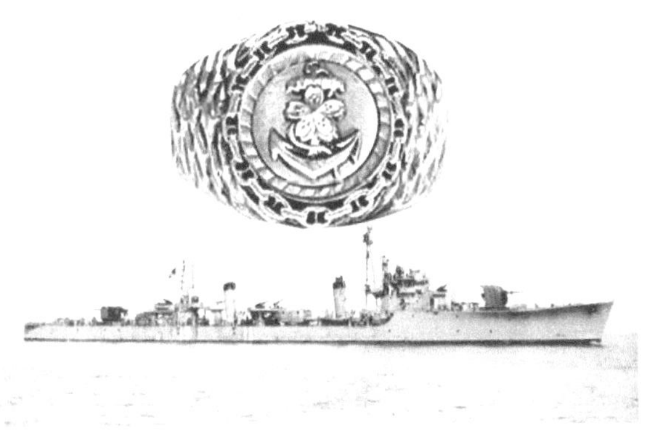

**The MATSU CLASS Japanese Supply
Destroyer Kaba-5055**

The Boy Who Rode The Dragon

**"Based on Actual Events in China
And Japan at the End of WWII"**

by
Ian Feldman

SSI Publishing, LLC
P.O. Box 815
Holly Springs, GA 30142
USA

Copyright 2024 © Ian Feldman

Table of Contents

PART ONE: THE LAST TRANSPORT

PART TWO: GOLD & TREASURE

PART ONE

THE LAST TRANSPORT

Chapter 1

The Destroyer Kaba-5505

In the final days of World War II, as Japan was evacuating China, Emperor Hirohito's nephew, Prince Nakahito authorized the secret transport of One-Thousand tons of gold and jewels to a temporary processing forge off the coast of Shandong, China.

OUR STORY BEGINS IN THE YELLOW SEA, NEAR THAT PLACE ON THE SOUTHEAST COAST OF CHINA:

Date: Mid-August, 1945

IT'S THE DARK OF NIGHT, AS A WIDER VIEW REVEALS THE DREADED. . .
Rising Sun Emblem of Japan's Navy. . .
Stitched into a flag, snapping above the Radar tower, in a stiff GALE from a hard Yellow Sea rainstorm.

Below it, glides the sleek hull of a MATSU CLASS Japanese Supply Destroyer. . . an Eighteen-Hundred Ton killer, cutting through the roaring spray.

INSIDE THE COMMAND DECK OF THE MATSU CLASS DESTROYER - KABA-5505:

COMMANDER EDO OZAWA pulls away from the controls. If you're fast, you can catch sight of a Naval Officer's 'RING', gold over black and silver.

In his hand is a coded document. He glances at it. It's a communiqué just received from their headquarters in Tokyo. He looks at his Executive Officer (XO) Kaname, then. . .

CLOSE UP: He focuses silently on the coded document as he speaks. . .

"EMPEROR HIROHITO HAS SURRENDERED IMPERIAL JAPAN TO THE ALLIES. . .

Make our boat - to all ahead SLOW, Depth - One-Hundred Meters, Kaname...
Position status?"

Executive Officer Kaname's expression is one of disbelief. . .

"Approaching Twelve-Thousand yards off the coastal entrance. Depth one hundred meters, Commander."

Commander Ozawa gazes at his watch. Ponders the sonar, longitude and latitudes numbers.

"Slow all engines to STOP, Kaname. . . Then assemble the entire crew in the forward storage hold."

The order travels down the chain of command, triggering an instant reaction of activity within the supply destroyer. The engines whirr to a deathly silence.

Commander Ozawa enters and faces the entire crew, now lined up below decks in the forward supply hold of the destroyer.

"Our Emperor tasked us with one of the most important missions of this war. Now we must choose to protect that mission, forever."

OUR EYES CREEP THROUGH the ship from the forward areas, to discover hundreds of WOODEN CRATES filled with looted gold and jewels from China. All of them lining the inside storage decks from the bow to the aft sections of the destroyer.

"It might come as a surprise to you, that we have now LOST the war."

Tension is everywhere, as murmurs travel throughout the crew members.

XO Kaname fires a sharp look at Ozawa: 'what are you doing?'   As Ozawa continues. . .

"We may have lost the war...but NOT our spirits. Make no mistake, Japan might be defeated, but Imperial Japan's people are not. Imperial Japan will rise again."

Commander Ozawa regards his crew with pride and duty. . . they are promising young men who have given everything for their country.

"It has been my esteemed honor to serve with you."

At once, with his right hand, Ozawa unsheathes his Naval Officers Dirk and places the blade at his gut, with his left hand he grabs a hidden wire, rigged with a button.

"To our families. May they remember us well. This one is straight from our Great Emperor Hirohito. . .
Banzai, Hirohito"

Suddenly, ALL the crewmen chant it together!
"Banzai. . . Banzai. . . Banzai!"

EXTERIOR TOP DECK VIEW:

The Destroyer thrashes on the black waves. Below deck you can almost hear the chorus screaming over and over 'Banzai' when -

. . . BAAM.

Within a millisecond, expansion and contraction -- a ball of fire engulfs the sky in burning air -- a burst that ends in an imploding suction of water below decks.

Bleeding air, fatally wounded, the metal beast sinks into the abyss, with a lament of steel...

Straight down into a watery grave Hundreds of meters below. . .

Chapter 2

Somewhere in Shanghai

WE ENTER INTO A PITCH BLACK SCENE:

PULL wider... from this close, it looks like canyons, valleys and rolling hills. Dim light shading them perfectly. . .

THEN WIDEN... A little more detail. A rough surface. Scratched. Like unfinished plaster.

WIDER STILL... And now we see it -- paint. Trapped under varnish. As a portrait begins to form... A dramatic rendition of a three-masted ship. . .   Caught in the furious swells at sea. Sailors trapped in the upturned waves, hands outstretched to heaven for salvation -- a painting in a gilded frame.

Another painting nearby. . . Noah's Arc trapped on the peaks of Mount Ararat.

Many more paintings. . . Aligning walls as our VIEW GROWS WIDER, we're inside . . . The 'Hall of Paintings' in a trendy Shanghai Maritime Museum.

Outside, it's windy. And the rustle of tree limbs against the building, adds to the eerie atmosphere.

Lamps throw dappled shadows across the hall.

The steady pulse of Mozart's Requiem pushes us through, as we explore.

When. . .

WHAM!

A man suddenly pushes past us. Throwing frenzied glances over his shoulder. . . At his pursuer.

But there's no one there. Just pools of unnerving shadows.

We see him more clearly now. Early 70's. Sprite for his age. Out of breath. Panicked. Meet PROFESSOR YAFENG ZHANG.

He clearly knows the Museum's layout, as he cuts into. . .

THE ARCHIVES

Running through canyons of shelves. Panic and fear merging with the rows of shelves. Growing into a confusion for him. This corner.

That row. Into another aisle. He turns a corner and SHWAP... He runs into. . .

A 'Man' holding a pistol straight at him.

The 'Man' has one ghastly discolored eye. And a stare that means business. . .

"Where is it?"

Nervously the professor reacts. . .

"I don't know w-w-what?"

The 'Man' seethes his words with vengeance.

"Where is it?"

A lethal sound that pushes the professor back. But Zhang won't be intimidated. . .

"It will take more than that."

The Man's vicious look, could kill a weaker person.

"I'm sure you're right."

The 'Man' holsters the Pistol inside his jacket. Then slides out an 8-inch-long 'Naval Dagger' sharpened to a suicidal point. The blade sings between them.

Finally, fear jumps out of Professor Zhang's eyes, as we torpedo in and crash to BLACK.

Then, as seen from beneath, KA-PLOOTCH!

The professor's head plunges into a bucket of water. Held there by a firm fist.

For a long time...

A time...until he stops fighting. His body now barely twitching. Like a lost S.O.S. at sea. . .

He succumbs.   Still, with eyes staring. . . wide-open. . . dull and dead.

There for all to see. . . the professor lays with his head in a bucket of water. In the middle of a room adorned with paintings and engravings of men who have died in 'China's Yellow Sea'.

Then we notice, the professor's Ring finger. It has been severed off. Leaving a blossoming pool of blood on the tiled floor.

LATER - OUTSIDE THE MUSEUM:

The same 'Man' is on his Cell Phone - digital reconnections take place down the line. Then Hong Kong ring tones. . .

On the other end, an 'English' accent picks up.

The 'Man' (now the 'Killer') . . . reacts into his Cell. . .

"It's done. And I have his 'Diary'."

The 'English' speaking voice replies. . .

"And the Professor?"

The 'Killer' is watching the paramedics carry the body out of the museum, zipped up in a body-bag, then lifting it into a waiting ambulance.

FORENSICS have already tagged the crime scene.

The 'Killer' grins his comment. . .

"As discussed."

Matter-of-fact, the 'English' voice replies. . .

"A Courier will gather the items at the appointed time. Then your fee will be transferred. . .
Also, I have one more task for you."

THE CELL CLICKS OFF. No goodbyes.

The 'Killer' tosses his 'burner phone' into a nearby canal. . . then walks down the street, disappearing through the gathering crowd. A murderer amongst the many, in the massive cityscape of Shanghai.

Chapter 3

Dadong Dao Island

SEVERAL FATHOMS UNDER DADONG DAO ISLAND:

At first, all is dark blue. Just the steady thrumming of a motor. Coming this way...

A NAUTICAL ROVER cruising, materializes from the dark at an Eight-Hundred Meter depth. Skimming the sandy bottom. A distinct 'Cone of Light' is trapping marine life and fauna in its beam.

It's an awe-inspiring kaleidoscope of coral and marine wildlife.

The world outside melts into an inky black. An alien probe in a strange land.

INSIDE INTERIOR OF A NAUTICAL ROVER:

We see a sticker that reads 'Divers do it Deeper', as we find the owner of the voice. . .

BOHAI XIANG. Sometime beach bum and history lover, sporting a tonic wheeler-dealer grin, that gets him out of trouble every time.

But mostly 'into' trouble, as he speaks. . .

"According to The British diary, we should be landing on the field of debris just about..."

PAPA NUI, Old Mandarin, best mate, early Fifties, too many pies and too much personality for one man, rocks the levers back and forth. Nothing gentle about this giant of a man.

And BANG...

They hit bottom with a sickening sound of metal. Bounce off. Everyone jerks around. Papa Nui fights with the whining hydraulics and finally steadies her.

As Bohai reacts, serious. . .

"Hey, hey-hey there."

Papa Nui comes back un-fettered. . .

"I knew motor-cross would come in handy."

On the monitor. A BLAST of silt, clouds everything. Drifting marine debris, distort the lens views. . .

Yet, they drive through it. Streams of images of the coral and sandy sea floor appear. Lots of it. But no signs of what Bohai's looking for.

Papa Nui continues to 'razz' him. . .

"I don't think you should buy your maps on eBay, Boss."

Bohai deflects! He's still focused. . .

"My maps are right."

More coral and rocky floor. The ground is beginning to sink toward the entrance of the 'Great' Abyss. . .
Papa Nui joshes him back. . .

"Google, maybe, but not eBay."

Bohai is still undeterred. . .

"Just, just give it a minute. . ."

Papa Nui suddenly gets serious. . .

Boss. . . we're approaching the GREAT 'A' ENTRANCE, dead man's drop. . .
Three-Thousand Meters of black nothing below us.
My insurance doesn't cover stupidity."

More, rocky floor. Desperation seeps in . . . And then. . . right there, Bohai catches sight of something, as he yells back. . .

"Wait, WAIT. . . There. Look."

Papa Nui releases the levers as the entire rover whirrs to a dead stop.

Bohai jabs the screen: Crusted, twisted fragments of metal poke out of the bedrock and coral heads. Like fingers of dead mariners reaching upward to the surface.

We push in on Bohai: His Eyes brighten up.

And soon...the skeleton frame of a . . .

SEA SURFACE - THE BATHYSPHERE SUPPORT SHIP – ON DECK:

Tight on GUOZHI HANG. A grizzled sea-salt millionaire who permanently has the best Cuban Cigar clenched between his teeth.

And now, he's red in the face and explodes!

"A 'Damn' fishing boat. . .that's all you found!

We're on the rear deck of Hang's – 'For Hire - Dive Support Ship', tricked up with all the latest deep sea exploration gadgets. The ROVER has been lifted on deck, dripping wet, the bottom covered in silt.

Bohai twists himself out of the hatch first, to face Guozhi Hang's ongoing harassment.

Then the two-man crew squeeze out right behind him, as Guozhi adds more. . .

"What the 'Hell" did you do to my Rover?"

Papa Nui shrugs a 'don't blame me' look, as Bohai fills in their answer. . .

"The geo-physics look the same. Same dimension. Same location. You know these things are not a Hundred. . ."

Guozhi breaks-in, with a new rant. . .

"At least give me a bib, if you're going to feed me anymore 'Bullshit'."

Bohai returns, with his best follow-up. . .

"It's here. The British and Imperial Admiral's 'Diary' spoke of a 'Matsu Class Destroyer' laden with gold, sunk at these precise coordinates."

From high above, we see they're just outside the inlet into Taiping Bay. We're on the southeast shore of Qingdao, China near the Yellow Sea.

Upon Guozhi's hand signal to the Bridge, the Support Ship begins moving Northwest to its home harbor near the Olympic Sailing Center.

Guozhi, then further inserts. . .

"Do you 'Idiots', even know how much money I've sunk in here?"

Without countering, Bohai starts regurgitating his best history distraction. . .

"In the last days of the war, the Imperial Navy sent a communiqué to Marshall Admiral Fushimi's Attaché in Tokyo, ordering him to release the Kaba, a Matsu Class Destroyer, on its mission out of Qingdao."

Guozhi's obviously frustrated with Bohai. . .

"This is why I was crazy, to take you on."

But, Bohai bullets on...

"WHY? They clearly had lost the war. As a final standoff? Patriotic fervor? No one knows the details of its mission. Only that it was loaded with 'Tons of Raw Gold Bullion and Jewels'.
Maybe over Five-Hundred Tons of it. . .
The point is, Japan was on the run, to GET out of China."

Bohai pauses, since he wasn't stopped. . .

"But the Prince and Hirohito were also planning a comeback. . .

And to do that, he needed MONEY. Negotiable and untraceable 'Gold Bullion Bars'."

"Okay, OKAY! I know the bedtime story, Bohai. . .
But it's not here. You need a better MAP!

"It's NOT a bedtime story, Guozhi. . .
The Destroyer Kaba was tasked directly by the Chief of Staff of the Imperial Japanese Navy. . .
Prince Fushimi himself."

"Listen, Call it a day, 'Dragon Rider'. The days of finding 'The Mystery Gold Bullion' are long GONE!"

"No, Guozhi. . . Listen. . . On Prince Fushimi's list, Only the 'Kaba' was considered unaccounted for. It was a specially designed 'Destroyer Supply Ship', built to carry serious additional tonnage over Two-Thousand miles. Plus, One-Thousand additional storage tons to be exact.
It was an Eighteen-Hundred Ton Destroyer. Maybe if we. . ."

"Bohai! Wake up, there's no other trip."

That breaks Bohai's momentum. He kicks at a deck board in frustration. One more try, 'shotgun' . . .

"On 15 August, 1945, in order to preserve the honor of the Imperial Navy, Prince Fushimi ordered the entire Japanese fleet scuttled, code name Golden Kite."

"Listen to me, Bohai...your first mistake is you put too much faith in 'fogged' history."

Bohai kicks loose without a breath. . .

"But at 1500 hours on August 16 Prince Fushimi was forced to withdraw this order, because Emperor Hirohito had agreed to the conditions of the 'Allied Unconditional Surrender'.

"Bohai...stop it. . . look..."

"But the Imperial Navy Admiral in the Sea of Japan believed this new surrender order to be against the Emperor's WILL, so he scuttled their vessels anyway."

"Bohai...we can't. . ."

"Guozhi, THINK! One-Hundred and Eight fully operational naval ships... '108'!
ALL, Scuttled in the Sea of Japan.
I want to go back to the archives. Maybe I've overlooked something. It's out there, somewhere.
'The Kaba' was NOT listed."

Finally, Guozhi Hang lets the 'Cat' out of the 'Bag'!

"I've been chartered, Bohai."

"No-wait-WHAT?"

"Bohai, an expedition out East of Okinawa down to the Coast of the Philippines, hired us for Three weeks. I'm leaving Monday."

"That means. . . WOW!
You're going to blow off the greatest 'Second World War Find' in history, for a fishing weekend?"

A body blow to Bohai. All he can do is stare, his mind racing for a way to salvage this.

Guozhi sincerely means it, as he tries to end the argument. . .

"It's been a pleasure..."

He shakes Bohai's hand, then starts to walk.

"Guozhi, you can't walk away from this."

Hang halts. . . then faces him.

"Give me ONE good reason and I won't."

Bohai just freezes in place. Mind racing. He can't think of a good reason.

Guozhi Hang waves him off. Bohai finds his crew watching him. Heads low. Sympathizing, as his First Mate chimes in . . .

"Boss. It's not so bad."

"What is?"

Quickly, Papa Nui adds his comic relief. . .

"Waxing surfboards. Umbrella drinks.
Beach 'Cheetahs' at the Sea Garden.
You're the Dragon! The Kitesurfing King!"

Nui goes serious. . .

"We had a good run, Boss."

As he shakes hands and goes below deck.

Just then, Bohai's Cell Phone rings. . . He waits. . . to think about what just happened. Bohai's eyes are cast to the sea. Where his prize still awaits him. . .

Chapter 4

The Interrogation

GOLDEN SANDY BEACH – QINGDAO, CHINA

AERIAL VIEW: We swoop over the boomerang-shaped peninsula, snug in its cerulean blue pocket of the Southern Yellow Sea. But on the horizon, a storm is brewing.

THERE RUSHING ALONG, we snag a 'Jeep'. Racing through 'desert-like' open country in a blur of sand, local trees and large aloe plants.

As we ease downward, we meet MEIFENG XIANG, at the Jeep's wheel. Beautiful, Forceful and Passionate.

She's got a stare that wills rock, with an intelligent gait that out-races any of her male counterparts.

Meifeng, intense, is on her Cell to Bohai.

"I'm out! Your Mother is driving me nuts. I can't stay restricted there! In that house with her, anymore, Bohai."

Just as quickly, she slams her Cell OFF.

DOWN THE COAST, AT SEA GARDEN BEACH:

We arrive at an azure blue 'horseshoe' bay surrounded on one side with restaurants, condos and hotels. Crawling through tourists we find Bohai, renting out umbrellas on the beach front.

He's finishing up with a 'Gorgeous Female' tourist from the Netherlands giving him a naughty, appreciative smile. . .

"By the way, I'm in Two-Twenty-Seven, here at the 'Sea Garden', interested?"

Bohai seems distracted, by other thoughts. . .

"I'm married, uh . . ."

She doesn't believe him. Thinks this just might be a hard-to-get flirtatious move. . .

"You're too young to be married. You're just a boy, are you not?"

Again, Bohai reacts, curiously. . .

"Married!   Happily, too. . . I think!?"

"And where is 'Mrs. Happily Married'?

She whispers in his ear. Bohai's eyebrows climb. Wow, that was dirty. Then resolute. . .

"Very married."

She GIGGLES. . .then smiles at him, as. . .
he watches her sashay away down the beach,
with a 'stupid grin' stapled to his face. Hmm-
hmm.

A man suddenly plants himself in Bohai's line
of vision.

DETECTIVE YUAN, a man born in a suit, who
looks more like an American FBI agent, than a
'Chinese Detective' on a summer beach front.

Bohai, tactfully drops his typical business line
on the Man . . .
"Five Dollars for the day or Thirty
Renminbi.   We have. . ."

"Bohai Xiang?"

"Who wants to know?"

INSIDE TERRACE - AT THE SEA GARDEN:

A little later. They're sitting under an
umbrella. Bohai's drinking a wild-fruit busting
cocktail. The Detective is drinking water, stoic
faced, as Bohai questions his intentions. . .

"Am I being interrogated?"

Detective Yuan, immediately hammers him. . .

"Everyone is a Suspect."

Bohai tries a little comedy. . .

"You'd get along great with my wife."

"Your ex-wife, as I'm aware. . ."

"We're not divorced."

Detective Yuan shrugs. . .

"Perhaps?"

Bohai jumps back in, knowing what's up. . .

"Look...Professor Zhang left a message a few days ago."

"Concerning?"

"I don't know. He wanted to meet. . .
Set the place and time. But he never showed.
I got caught up with a dive, so I forgot to call him back."

"You forgot?"

"Okay, so we don't get along."

"Ever since the separation?"

"Father-in-laws can be funny that way."

Bohai pauses. . .

"I'm a little fuzzy. . . what's the purpose of your visit, again?"

Detective Yuan slides a few crime scene photographs in front of Bohai. Bohai deflates.

"Can you see anything irregular?"

"Other than the last time I saw him he was alive...No."

Another picture. Bohai's jaw muscles twitch.

"Now?"

Bohai looks, then shakes his head. . .

"No."

"And now. . ."

Bohai looks again, shakes 'No'. then. . .

"No wait. Something's missing. . . His finger. His 'RING'. . ."

Detective Yuan shifts uncomfortably, now his attention is completely focused on Bohai.

"Yeah. Humm... it had an inscription. . . Japanese or German from WWII?
He found it on an excavation inside a 'Naval Yard', near Incheon, Korea."

"Do you know what was on it?"

Bohai thinks hard. But can't remember.

"It was an 'Imperial Naval Officer's RING'."

Bohai plays off Yuan's puzzled look. . .

"You know. . . 'A Japanese Naval Commander'. World War II? Don't you read history?

The Third Reich forged them specifically for certain Officers of 'Japan's Imperial Navy'."

Bohai waits for a reaction. . . None.

"Hard Twenty-Carat Gold-On-Silver. . .
These 'RING's were hand-crafted like the 'Waffen SS and Reichmarine', but were never officially issued by Japan.
Only 'Imperial Naval Officers' that served on German bases like Penang were given these."

Bohai wants to say more, but stops. Yuan catches on...

"Except...?"

"Except at the end of the war, when certain commanders of select 'Destroyer' crews were issued these 'RINGS' for their last Missions. . .
Like 'Evacuating Loot' stolen from mainland China and Korea."

"Ah, the Dragon Gold myth. . . 'The General Yamashita's Gold'.

"Not a myth. . ."

Detective Yuan packs up the photos, stands to leave.

"General Yamashita was in the Philippines, not China.
'Dragon Gold' was never taken from China. If had been, someone would have found it by now."

He looks at Bohai for reaction. . .then adds.

"Besides MacArthur and the Americans probably found 'Yamashita's Gold' hideout in the Philippines or Japan, then secretly hid it or took it back to their New York Banks for themselves."

"No. Something happened to that final mission. Prince Nakahito issued the orders, but the final location has always been elusive."

"What makes you think that, Mr. Xiang?"

"British records and Imperial Naval Diaries were destroyed at War's End. So no one knows where to start?"

"My point exactly: No records, No treasure, more foolish speculation."

Bohai's mind is racing. Possibilities igniting behind his stare.

"What if, whoever did this to Professor Zhang is after the 'Dragon Gold and Jewelry' looted from China, themselves?"

"We think it was a crime of opportunity."

"But nothing was stolen. . . was it?"

Yuan grimaces. This is a sticking point in his investigation. And damn Bohai for picking up on it.

Then Detective Yuan, puts one last photograph on the table.

"Near the black forensic marker on the floor, Professor Zhang wrote. . .
            'HT-09-12-72...Bohai...'
Then, the writing trails off. . .
Do you know the meaning of the letters and numbers in this photo, Mr. Xiang?"

Bohai can hardly talk. He's shocked. Shakes his head. . .

"No I can't."

"Why would He, write YOUR name?"

"Maybe he was trying to warn me or something. I don't know."

And then, a thought occurs to him -

"What if markings on the 'RING' lead to the treasure?"

The Detective shakes his head. . .

"I'll be in touch, Mr. Xiang."

As he walks away. . .

Bohai shouts back at him. . .

"Professor Zhang wasn't the target."

Yuan pauses a moment. Stays in profile, as Bohai nails in his final point.

"And he won't be the last."

Yuan let's it sink in. Salutes, then leaves.

Chapter 5

Imperial Naval Officer's Ring

Imperial Naval Officer's Ring

THE BEACH FRONT AT QINGDAO: The blood burst of the setting sun, colors the entire sky. We favor the marina below, where Bohai is marching up the pier. . .

THE MARINA: Bohai hurries toward the lights from Hang's Support Ship. Just as, Papa Nui rushes toward him and Bohai yells back. . .

"What's the big emergency!"

"Heard YOU and Meifeng are getting divorced."

"We're not getting divorced, Papa!"

"Boss, you're not going to believe this. . ."

HANG'S SUPPORT SHIP: They both march toward the 'ROVER', suspended by cables and resting on a rack, as Bohai questions. . .

"I thought you'd shipped out! Left on 'Hang's Big Trip' already. . .

"Over here, Boss."

They gather under the ROVER. The bottom is still caked with silt and coral sand.
Papa Nui dumps his load. . .

"You know that bump we hit at the bottom?"

"Yeah, so what?"

"I just wanted to say, that I think it's great that you're NOT getting divorced."

"Would you get off my back about this, Papa. We're not getting divorced."

"Okay. Cause you make a great couple. You're both stubborn as mules, but great mules together."

Bohai cringes.

"That doesn't make any sense."

"Okay. Okay. The bump, right? I thought we had punched through. But, I found this, caught in the cabling. . ."

Papa Nui produces a 'severed mummified' man's hand. Incrusted in Coral gunk.

"You gotta be kidding me."

"I nearly chucked my diner, Boss."

"Is this real?"

"That's not the cool part?"

"There's a cool part?"

Papa Nui invites Bohai to lay on a creep-board under the 'ROVER Bathysphere'.
And there, on their backs flashlights in hand, they stare up at a . . .
Metal gash scraped across the bottom.

"Damn, I can't afford to fix this, Papa."

Papa Nui smiles at Bohai.

"Too bad Meifeng's not here to see this. She loves all that 'ghoulish stuff'."

"Nui..."

"Now pay attention, Boss. Stop interrupting. Look closer."

Bohai fixes on the gash. Then, slowly, like fireworks, his eyes brighten, then puzzle. . .

"Boss, it's not even the same metal as the damn ROVER. That's something we picked up. It's. . ."

"Metal from another boat?"

"Disco, Boss!"

"And not a fishing boat, Papa?"

"Tha'd be my guess!"

They stare at each other with giddy wonder. . .
As together, they both shout!

"A Naval Boat?! A Destroyer?!"

"You mean we were right on top of it?"

"Or something that belongs to it, Boss."

"Wait a minute, wait a 'Damn Minute'. We
need to go back."

"Guozhi wants your 'HEAD' on a stick."

"We gotta convince him, Papa."

"Hey, what's this 'WE' stuff."

They roll out from under the 'ROVER'.

"We're fully chartered in the morning for the
Philippines."

Bohai pinches his lips into a tight line. 'Damn'.
Papa Nui fixes him with a cheeky stare.

"There just might be a way to convince Guozhi
that you're not a 'total waste' of a treasure
hunter."

"Good luck with that."

Papa Nui lifts up the 'HAND' between them.
His thumb rubs out muck around part of one
finger.

Something underneath catches the light.
Something shiny. Bohai looks closer.
Suddenly, his Face blossoms into an open
circle of stunned shock.
He's staring at a . . .
'Silver Chrysanthemum over an Anchor' in a
solid disk of Twenty-Carat Gold.
It's an actual Imperial Navy 'Chrysanthemum
Throne' Officers 'RING'.

"Can you read the markings inside?"

"No! It's in German. I thought it would be in
Japanese. But with Qingdao's German
influence, how hard can it be to translate it,
right here in town?"

An eerie wind picks up, blowing in a creeping
fog, as if a 'Thousand Ghosts' from the past
precipitously spawned from the depths. . .

The Royal Dutch Bank in Shanghai

Chapter 6

Royal Dutch Bank - Shanghai

**INSIDE A PRE-WWII ENGLISH MANOR –
SHANGHAI: Hurried footsteps march over
marble floors and through oak paneled rooms.**

**We only catch glimpses. Expensive cuff links.
Italian shoes. Crisp silk shirt...
The 'Courier' is holding a small box in his right
hand.
He enters the vast library. Rare first editions
and Century-Old books wallpaper the room
along with multiple Chinese artifacts and
Korean Joseon Dynasty blue and white
porcelain celadon glazed jars. . .**

The 'Courier' stops at a large wing back chair.
The 'Executive Occupant' we don't see, takes
the box.
And then we see it for the first time. An
'Imperial Japanese Naval War Diary'.
Two swords and an anchor circled by a chain
on its hard cover.
And the 'Chrysanthemum of Hirohito' is
centered on its yellowed leather.

The 'Executive Occupant' opens the Diary. And
there finds a black and white picture of the
Official 'Imperial Navy Chrysanthemum
RING'.

Also, a schematic drawing points out other
details of the Twenty Rings, custom made in
1943 for Prince Nakahito of Imperial Japan.
He concentrates on the inscription inside the
'RING'. Turning the next several pages, it
reveals the details and hull design of Twenty
'MATSU CLASS Japanese Supply Destroyers'
set for specific recovery missions: GOLD
BULLION.

Then it gets to the Imperial Japanese Officer's
list. Each Officer is detailed with his assigned
'RING' Numbers and Initials. The 'Executive
Occupant' then closes the Diary and smiles to
himself.

He peers from behind the wingback. Pale,
cold, empty eyes. A hard jawline. A Pure
corporate climber. The 'Executive Occupant' is
VANBOVEEN. And for those of you who have
paid attention, he was the 'English Voice' at
the end of the phone.
Vanboveen, then barks out his orders. . .

"Notify Haughton, in Hong Kong!"

A HONG KONG ESTATE: We climb up a massive amount of stairs winding up to a mountain top estate with a helicopter pad near a broad entrance overlooking all of Victoria Harbour and the main cityscape.

The garden is an 18th century English styled garden masterpiece that stretches almost two tennis courts wide. More a tapestry of art then a horticultural expanse.

In a grove of Bonsai trees, we find SYDNEY HENRY HAUGHTON. Sixties, Icy blue eyes. Gentle manner. Tenderly snipping leaves into a basket. A manservant approaches him...

"Sir, they have called a meeting."

Haughton's head drifts in thought. 'Now that's interesting. . .'

"That can only mean one thing."

The manservant comes to attention...

"Prepare my jet!"

ROYAL DEUTSCHE BANK OF SHANGHAI: This place is NOT what you would think of as, one the most powerful banks in the world.

Not a gaudy steel and concrete high-rise tower, but a well-appointed English, Edwardian brick mansion in the City Centre of Shanghai directly connected to Citibank in New York and the Banque Privée de Rothschild S.A in Geneva Switzerland.

Its well-tended grounds are shaded by high walls and manicured trees. Not a car in the lot under $250,000 USD.

We overhear, the sage voice of Haughton. . . English with a slight German accent.

"You've put us at risk. Anyone who touches any part of this, must disappear permanently."

THE BANK'S ATRIUM: We creep through the corridors of power. Oak paneling. Black marbled floors. Money and Power evidenced everywhere. Suited corporate league types silently dip in and out of offices. Marching toward. . .THE BOARDROOM.

"Time is critical. Our sister firms in New York, London, Luxembourg and Banque Privée in Geneva will want immediate closure."

ROYAL DEUTSCHE BOARDROOM: Close-up, Sydney H. Haughton. Piercing all seeing eyes. But a purposely calming voice. Short on legs, but big on power. Make no mistake; behind his apparent gentleness, lurks the shark's instinct for blood driven by pure evil.
Every single member of the Board around the table is silently petrified of him.
A wall video monitor streams financial data. Seated, we find VanBoveen waiting. At Fifty, he's a Corporate Boardroom veteran, a
ROYAL DEUTSCHE BANK lifer, Haughton's "go to" boy.
Haughton turns to him.
"Solve this quickly. No media.
Especially where the Chinese Government is concerned."

VanBoveen nods. It will be done. VanBoveen hands Haughton, 'Zhang's Diary' pointing to the last entry. Haughton reads it.

"The appearance of an 'Imperial Naval Officer's RING' means one thing!"

He pauses, as he re-checks 'Zhang's Diary' entry again.

"A 'MATSU CLASS Destroyer' is somewhere under one of 'Three Coastal Islands' East of Qingdao. Now we must find out, which one!"

On the wall screen, the financial details disappear. A black and white picture of the Imperial Naval Officer's 'RING' with German inscription. Schematic drawings point out details.

"The names of Prince Nakahito's select Officers on these 'Gold Bullion' ships were etched, as three letter initials on each 'RING'."

Haughton again pauses. . .scans the room.

"Japan kept meticulous records. Those that were not destroyed by MacArthur, are in our Swiss Vaults."

Haughton holds up the yellowed 'Imperial Naval Diary'.

"If any of the initials in this 'Diary' are present on this 'Naval Officer's Ring', then we have our target. Do we have the 'RING'?"

VanBoveen cues two security operatives to hand over the box to Haughton.

Haughton pulls out the 'RING'.

Examines it in the half-light under a camera lens. The 'RING' appears on the wall screen. A murmur of astonishment travels the room. We recognize the 'RING' as the Professor's 'RING' in the opening scene. Haughton's keen eye sweeps over the details.

"Late 1943 design, I should venture. Solid Silver and Twenty-Carat Gold center. Uncirculated. It matches the catalogue. Definitely the Imperial Navy type we are looking for."

He reads the inscription with interest. A curious little smile blossoms on his face...
...The room takes its cue; the smile travels the room.
This is good news.
Haughton reads out the inscription with a full baritone German accent, as we concentrate on the inscription inside the 'RING'.

"Fick dich, Nazi der drecksack."

Haughton clears his throat, as he pauses before his English translation. . .

"Fuck you, 'Dirty Nazi Bastard."

Stunned silence, throughout the ROOM.

"The Professor has a sense of humor. . .
This Meeting is OVER!"

Everyone streams out of the room. Taking with them, a shock of disbelief.

"VanBoveen!"

Not a man to show fear, VanBoveen swallows hard. When the last person leaves. . .

"Nice little snafu. I have a family member whom I think you would like."

Haughton faces VanBoveen. . .

"KSK Exkommando & British SAS. Obedient. Wants to join the family trade. I should think you would find good use for a true 'Black Ops' member. And very good at cleaning up, too."

VanBoveen nods. He understands.

"Right away, Sir."

"And no more mistakes. Though this one was highly entertaining, I don't have the patience for another.
Oh, and terminate that 'RING Courier' that killed the Professor...
He throws the 'RING' over to VanBoveen, who catches it in midflight.

"Where will I find your, Operative . . .

Haughton smiles. But it never reaches his eyes. And it sends a shiver down VanBoveen's spine.

"She'll find you."

Chapter 7

Bohai and Meifeng

GOLDEN SANDY BEACH: Meifeng is nervously tapping her GOLD wedding band against the steering wheel of her Jeep.
Her thoughts miles away.
Suddenly annoyed, she jerks the 'RING' off onto the floorboard. Then kicks it into a rug hole. A pile of documents flaps in the wind on the passenger seat. Bursting with post-it notes and scribbles.
And we catch one word -- "Divorce".

Solid, leaden clouds shuttle overhead. The Winds have picked up. Sweeping trees and Sea swells are impacted by the intense wind.

While everyone is coming out of the water, sailors mooring their boats to the pier. . .

Meifeng throws caution in the air and walks straight toward the sea. Clad in her diving suit, she's arguing with a LOCAL FISHERMAN trying to pull his boat away from the oncoming Ocean horror. . .He's shouting at her. . .

"Weatherman say, it's the biggest storm for a hundred years, coming!"

Meifeng doesn't listen. . .

"Take me out there."

"I can't do that. You our friend, Meifeng!"

"Just drop me off. I'll find my way back."

"These waters unpredictable. You get turned around and never come back, Meifeng."

Lightning cracks the horizon. Thunder rolls.

"One-Thousand Renminbi."

By the look of the old man, his ragged shirt, a Thousand Renminbi is a lot of money. This is torturing him. . .

"Why you can't wait after the storm?"

Rain begins to beat on her face. Meifeng has a crazed look behind her eyes, as she stares him into reacting. As if challenging the gods, she shouts at him. . .

"Because, this is TREASURE weather."

Then, as if in reply from the gods, lightning forks overhead.

Challenge accepted. . .

DEEP WATER - OFF GOLDEN SANDY BEACH: Underwater -- WHOOSH. Meifeng dives in.

She's sinking into another world.

Propellers overhead, cut a beeline for the shore. Waves batter the surface. Churning the water-world. This is no place for anyone to be, yet. . .
Meifeng dives toward the blue abyss. Cruising along the sinking slope. Eyeing her wrist compass and gauges.

The underwater world is no quieter than on the surface above.
Waves batter the coral outcrops. The bracing current churns up plant life and silt.
Meifeng is beating and pushing against the pressure.
Her wet suit holding back the cold.
The current is shifting the sand and coral bottom. Pushing aside great slabs of sea floor.

Then THWAP...
A massive coral trunk smacks into her. Sends her reeling.
Quickly, she recovers and is back in. Looking for her spot.
And then, there below. . .
The almond shape of a boat pressed down by centuries of water and current, finally exposes itself.

She swims to a solid coral outcrop. Pulls a rope from around her waist, then ties it around the coral monster, to create her life-anchor.

This is one scary place to be.
Half the ocean is black, as it comes towards her, dropping into the abyss, then changing all at once from clear blue to BLACK.
The other Half is whirling in a storm of water, sand and coral debris.

Meifeng seems to surfs in it. . . trailing the current at the end of her rope, she dodges debris.
But true enough...the seabed beneath her is eroding. It Chips away, Fast.
Exposing beams of wood. Manmade. Flat.
Nailed together by wooden studs.

She pulls herself to the sandy bottom and
begins digging.
Plunging her dagger. Prying up silt.
Then -- TINK!

She salvages a gold cup from a bed of gold
ingots. Bingo. She scoops the lot into her side-
bag just as. . .
A bull shark looms out from the murk.
She focuses on that stealthy, slithering
silhouette.
About five meters away. Seconds to her, if it
decides to rush her.
Meifeng's eyes grow wide, watching. And
gently, she tightens the side-bag. Keeping her
eyes on the shark. Then her knife! She slices
through the rope and
WHOOOSH...

Like a 'Jet Express', she's sucked back into the
pushing current. A rapid elevator-ride back
toward the shore.
And just as fast, the sea bed shifts, obliterating
all traces of the wreck and remaining treasure.

Meifeng streamlines into the current. Beating
away in a graceful dolphin kick, melting into
the turmoil. . .shore bound.

HANG'S SUPPORT YACHT: Later that afternoon on Board the Yacht at the Marina, we see Meifeng and Guozhi Hang haggling. . .

"Five years in the planning; one hour in the execution, Guozhi . . ."

"She is a beauty, no doubt about it, Gal."

We see a WIDER VIEW on Meifeng's horde of TREASURE.
Spread on a cloth. Polished to a twinkle. Intricately carved golden cups. Gold Ming Dynasty coins. Antique Chinese jewelry.

"Same arrangement as before?"

"My contact at the museum will take them, no questions. I'll wire the payment, Meifeng."

He appraises the find again.

"The Chinese Government will be pleased to see their heritage back."

"Keep my name out of it, as before. You file the Government Docs, I'll just do the dirty work."

Guozhi Hang nods: 'will do'.

Meifeng wanders away from the treasure to a wall map. Her eyes scan the tiny islet of Dadong Dao.   Searching for that elusive treasure. . .

"Are you, positive she's out there, Meifeng?"

"Her and her sisters.

There's also likely some 'Matsu Class Destroyers' out there too, with even more Multi-Millions maybe even Billions in Gold and Jewels. And I'll find them too."

"Others have tried, Gal."

Ah, there it is. . . she was wondering when the conversation would turn to Bohai.

"Bohai's not looking in the right places."

"Bohai's leaving Qingdao, you know. For the Singapore, I heard. A semi-emotional panic..."

"I might have heard that, Guozhi. But, why are you telling me that?
I know that. It's not like I would follow him... we're through."

"Right! And I know that too. Don't you think, I know that. . . I know that."

Guozhi adds, as an afterthought. . .

"He knows his stuff, though."

"He knows "History", Guozhi."

"He knows "Treasure", too."

"He's got no 'Instinct'. Not for Treasure. Not for Women, either!"

"That little stunt on the reef, Gal, that was good."
He pauses for emphasis. . .
"Phenomenal, in fact!

When I'm old with a few golf balls floating loose upstairs, it'll be the story I'll tell my grand-kids. . .
But in the end, Gal, 'Instinct' is not enough. Not in this game. It can get you killed."

We ZOOM in on Meifeng's face. Thinking about that, the map reflecting in her eyes.

Suddenly, Three-horn blasts announce the departure of Guozhi ship. . .

ON DECK… Meifeng's triple-checking her equipment, spread out on deck.
But, something on the dock below catches her attention.
It's Bohai. Running toward them. Meifeng leans over the bulwark -

"You running free again, Bohai?"

Bohai skids to a halt on the Dock. There's no way he can catch the ship. All he can do is stand there, hand raised in the air --holding something. . .

Meifeng squints into the brightness blocking her view.

"What the …"

She fishes and finds binoculars. Zooms in on Bohai's hand. Suddenly the 'Imperial Naval RING' grows to life.
Glinting in the sun.

"No way."

She zooms in closer.

"WTF! Really? No!"

"No way."

Her face finally settles on 'Shit'...

"This better not be a trick, Bohai Xiang. . .
We're not getting back together."

Then Meifeng loses it. . .

"Stop the ship!"

Bohai hops onboard. Guozhi Hang's red in the
face.

"You dumped me for her, Guozhi? When did
this happen?

"This better not be a desperate attempt to. . ."

Bohai chucks something at him, cutting him
off, something Guozhi Hang fumbles like a hot
Ping-Pong ball. The 'RING'.
Shiny in his hand. His face blossoms.

Meifeng is pissed. . .

"Get off my ship.
We're leaving in 15 minutes."

Hang passes it to Meifeng, cutting her off. She
stares hard. Flips it back and forth.
Struggling not to be impressed, as she says. . .

"The things you find at the flea market."

"Not the flea market. On a 'Dive', Meifeng!"

"You could only have found this inside a 'Matsu Class Destroyer' Hull, Bohai!"

"Bingo."

"And if you found a 'Matsu Class Boat', you found. . .

"Right on! Treasure, DRAGON TREASURE."

"But you don't have treasure."

"No...b-but...I've got the location of the treasure.

"The actual location?"

"Well...roughly."

Guozhi Hang immediately interrupts. . .

"Great. We stopped my ship for 'roughly'."

Meifeng is now really angered. . .

"Get off my charter."

"Whoa, wait. It was mine before you stole it."

Hang again, jumps in . . .

"She booked it, before you did."

Now Guozhi cringes; he's said 'too much'.

Bohai throws his hands up; 'Great, another Betrayal'. . . then drops a serious reaction. . .

"You knew about this all along, Guozhi?"

"It doesn't matter, WHAT I knew.
You came up empty handed. I've got mouths to feed."

Bohai snaps the 'RING' back. . .

"Not empty-handed -- an actual hand!"

Meifeng jerks in her reaction. . .

"What?"

Bohai waves her off; 'too complicated'; he's on a roll. . .as Guozhi Hang comes back. . .

"You'll need to translate those markings."

"This is the first 'RING' to surface in Sixty Years, Guozhi. We're getting closer to solving it!"

There's a crazed fever in Bohai's eyes that infects both Guozhi Hang and Meifeng, just as Papa Nui walks up babbling to Guozhi Hang.

"See, I told you they were 'Grrreat' together!"

But Meifeng snaps out of it; she knows where Bohai is heading with this. . .

"No, No, No! Absolutely, No!"

Bohai pleads directly to Hang. . .

"I only need somebody who can read the 'Lay of the Land', Guozhi."

Papa Nui points to both of them jokingly, then smiles. . .as Hang remarks. . .

"You do have incredible 'Instinct', Bohai!
. . . Ah screw the grand-kids, I'm in . . .
Get the boat ready Nui!"

Papa Nui rushes off, as Bohai suddenly STOPS Cold, notices the table with Meifeng's Treasures laid out. . .

"Ah, Wow!   . . . Awesome, Meifeng!
'Chinese Dragon' Loot, from the war?!"

"Japanese Torpedo Boat! 'The Kasasagi'."

"Cool. . . 'The Kasasagi'. South, huh!?"

Unexpectedly, Meifeng drifts next to him.

"Half a click off. . . Southwest."

"On a skiff?"

"Like you 'Researched' it; where you said it would be. . . Off Golden Sandy Beach."

Unconsciously, they draw closer. More intimate.   A 'Mutual Interest' bonding them. Truly, a glimpse of how exciting they must have been together in a 'Previous Life'.

"Then the 'War Legends' WERE True!"

There's still 'Passion Here'. For Treasure. And Maybe 'For Each Other'. . .
Without warning, Meifeng 'Breaks the Spell' -

"Goddammit. You always do this!

You are the ONE, that always hijacks my plans."

Meifeng storms over to her backpack. She's Rummaging furiously. . .
Then 'JERKS' out a stack of paper. . .

As Bohai crudely, tries to salvage the moment.

"It's a good plan. Just mine's better."

THEN. . . Slams Bohai in the chest with it.

"I'm your 'New Partner', Bub!"

AS . . . She storms OUT, Yelling. . .

"After you sign all 'The Arrows'."

Bohai stares, LOST, at the pile of papers. 'Divorce Documents'. A devastating discovery. His signature required where all the 'Arrows' Point.

He takes in a deep breath. 'At what point did his life take such a Wrong Turn?'

ONSHORE AT THE MARINA: Unknown to all of them, 'The Killer' is watching Hang's Support Ship moored at the dock. . .

There's a frenzy of activity on deck. He dials VanBoveen's number. . .
Nothing.
After a moment, the line goes dead.

'The Killer' comments to himself. . .

'Screw it! Gotta get that 'RING' this time or I'm dead!'

He reaches into his Car's Glove compartment. Slips on a pair of 'Black Assassin Gloves'. . . Screws on a Silencer to his 'Beretta M9A' and grins!

MUCH LATER THAT DAY - A BACK-ROAD TO SHANGHAI: Bohai's 'Red Toyota' is gliding down the gently curving country road. Sunset is glowing on the western mountain horizon. . . effectively casting a silhouette on the low valleys. . .as Bohai glances over to his uncooperative passenger. . .

"Your Dad mentioned a 'Diary', where he wrote all of his life research."

Meifeng watches the countryside glide by. She's lost in thoughts. . .

"Much good it did him. He never found any of the sunken Destroyers."

Bohai focuses on the road ahead, while casually changing the subject. . .

"We need to get this 'RING' translated. And match it up against the German records, Meifeng. . ."

She spits back, at him. . .

"The German records are useless. We need the 'Imperial Navy's List'. It's the KEY; without that KEY, No Secret. 'No Dragon Gold'."

Up ahead, a CAR is angled across the road. A motorcycle overturned in the center.

An accident. A man frantically flags him down.

Bohai pulls down the window when. . .
A 'Beretta 9 mm' presses against his temple, 'snagging' his complete attention. . .

"Get out of the car."

Bohai shows no sign of moving, mind racing for an escape. The 'so called injured' Motorcyclists runs around to Meifeng's side. Knocks on the glass; she won't lower the window.

WWHAACK!
He smashes it in, with a great shower of glass. Grabs her by the hair, and bodily yanks her out of the car.
Then stands her in front of the car and presses his 'Pistol' to her head. . . for Bohai to see.

It's subtle. A flash of 'bizarre' communication, between 'Bohai's Gunman' and the 'Motorcyclist'.

'Bohai's Gunman' is stunned: 'What are you doing, you Idiot?'
The 'Motorcyclist' ignores him as Bohai reacts.

"Okay, Okay. I don't have any. . ."

"We want the 'RING', ASSHOLE!"

"The what. . ."

THWACK.

The 'Gunman' nails Bohai across the temple with the grip of his Beretta.

Sending a sharp, hot pain through his forehead.

"Oh my GOD!   Fine. . . it's in the glove compartment."

He moves toward the glove compartment, very slowly. . .

"Can I?"

The 'Gunman' tightens his grip on his Pistol.

"Go get it. . ."

Bohai dives into the passenger side and catches a glimpse of a terrified Meifeng, shaking her head: 'don't do it'.

"Hurry up, ASSHOLE. . ."

At his glove compartment, Bohai rummages around for the 'RING'. Pulls out a cloth which he hands over to the 'Gunman'.

Bohai locks a stare with Meifeng. A silent communication that says: 'be ready'.

As the gunman walks to the Motorcyclists and shows him the 'RING', Bohai stomps the accelerator. . .
The car bolts forward.
Slams into them -- Meifeng dives out of the way. . . as Bohai YELLS. . .

"Jump in!"

Meifeng barely has time to vault into his Toyota, with Bohai reversing it. Foot to the metal. Engine screaming in a tortured high-pitch. Bohai spins the wheel. Does a 'One-Eighty', then grinds the gears into forward and peels out.

Putting as much distance between him and their deadly danger as possible, Bohai continues to 'gun-it'. They're apparently fast enough, as the baddies disappear in the rearview mirror. . .

Shocked, Meifeng opens up. . .

"Who were those 'Bastards'?"

"Are you okay? You're okay, right?"

"Yes, Yes. Just a little shook-up. . . What do you think that was about?"

"Are they behind us, Meifeng?"

"Not after what you did there!"

A heart-beat, as they let that sink in. It might be nerves, it might be adrenaline, it might fear. . . but thrilled, smiles blossom on both their faces.

"That was WILD!"

"I know, right. . . You know Bohai, I thought I'd be a bit more freaked out, having a GUN to my head. . . Damn, it was a loaded GUN, too!"

"They know about the 'RING', Meifeng!"

At once, images finally start flushing into her mind.

"Oh MOTHER, I'm gonna be sick."

"You don't know the half of it, Meifeng. . ."

"What?"

Bohai cuts the Toyota into another country road, heading South once again. . . and purposely avoiding the answer.

"Bohai, you've got that look. . .What have you done?"

"Look in the glove compartment."

She does. Catches her breath. Pulls out the 'Imperial Navy 'RING'.

"But... you gave them a Ring. I saw a Ring.

"You saw 'A GOLD RING'. I substituted my gold engagement Ring, for the 'RING'!"

"You substituted your engagement Ring? I gave you that. . ."

She doesn't know whether to kiss him or punch him. She's conflicted. Hurt. Bohai sees it instantly.

"I -- I didn't know it mattered. . . now.
I had to do something, QUICK."

Trying to convince herself. . .

Meifeng stares at him. . .

"You're right -- you're right! It doesn't matter.
It. Doesn't. Matter. Now."

"That's right."

"Right!"

Long, hanging pause. . .

"I can't believe you keep your Ring in the car --
Who does that?"

"Meifeng, really?   What did you EXPECT!"

Turning into a sharp bend in the road. . .
the Toyota disappears toward Shanghai. . .
cloaked by the growing darkness of NIGHT. . .

A SHANGHAI ROOF TOP-NEAR MIDNIGHT:
Panoramic views of the cityscape at night are
filled with pools of shadows everywhere.

We crawl to find a 'SNIPER'. Nearly invisible.
Tucked behind a fire-ladder. Rifle pointed --

SNIPER SCOPE VIEW: Through crosshairs,
three street thugs below. Horsing around.
Waiting.
Suddenly we recognize 'Bohai's GUNMAN'.
It's a dingy alleyway. The three thugs pace.
Wasting time when. . .
The 'Professor's Killer' finally arrives. Just a
shadow at the other end of the alley.

SNIPER SCOPE VIEW AGAIN:
Crosshairs are now on the Killer. Slow, calm
footsteps. His shadow tacked at the heels. The
scope tracks him. . .

'The Sniper' pulls away from the scope.
Hmmm...rethinks a new strategy.

Below, the Killer approaches 'Bohai's
Gunman'. . . who speaks with vengeance.

"You said this was gonna be easy.
A walk in the park. . . They were both a
'menace', crazy boy. . .crazy girl."

'The Killer' eyes 'Bohai's Gunman'
suspiciously. . .

"Do you have it?"

'The Gunman', spits it out. . .

"Yeah, I got it.

But I think we should renegotiate our deal. . .
For the inconveniences, we suffered. . .
Know what I mean."

'The Killer' stares at 'Bohai's Gunman'. . .

"Show me."

'The Gunman', goes tuff. . .

"Nah. First, your appreciation! Show me some
'Red Mao's'. . . And then you'll see. . .

TZIP-TZIP-TZIP. . .

One smoldering black bullet hole in the head,
two in the heart.
So fast, this move only has a beginning and an
ending.
Tattooing a stunned expression on
'The Gunman's' face as he goes down, splat. . .

"Shit!"
In unison, the other two thugs barely have
time to move. . .

TZIP-TZIP. . .

Two shots and they're down. No aiming.
Just pure instinct. Invisible bullets tack them
in the back of the head.
Punching out their faces. . .

Crimson clouds of mist evaporate in the dank
alley air.
'The Killer's' measured steps stand by the
bodies, as he. . .

TZIP-TZIP. . .

Double taps. In each head. Impact twitching
the corpses.
Violent, remorseless, sickening.

'The Killer' walks to the lifeless body of
'Bohai's Gunman'.
Searches him. Finds the 'RING'.

Unrealized, it's 'Bohai's Gold Wedding Ring'.

He wraps it up, but. . . his sixth sense. . .
kicks in . . . and he only completes half a turn,
When...SCHLICK. . .From behind. . .
A thin wire tightens around his neck. Catching
his arm between the wire and his neck.
Fast. Violent. Totally unexpected.

He struggles to spin. The attacker's too agile.
Whips his right elbow back. . . can't reach him.
ARRGGHH, the wire lacerates the soft flesh of
his forearm. . .
Starts SAWING!
Pain fires through his arm. He barely reaches
in his coat for his silenced Beretta. . .

TZIP-TZIP-TZIP.
Fires through the inside. Punching holes in
the back of his coat. Two go wide -- one
connects. . .

It recoils the unexpected, 'Sniper'.
'The Sniper' clutches the bleeding leg.
This gives 'The Killer' a wide enough gap to
slide out of the wire.

Then facing his opponent. . .
Not a Man . . . a Woman. Eastern European.
In her twenties. Muscular. Very attractive.

Coiled like a cobra. Limping.
Meet 'HANNA'.

'The Killer' shakes off the confusion. 'WTF?'

Shouts at her . . .

"Who sent you?"

'Hanna' steps up to his body. . .
Then click...click-click. . .
'The Killer' fires empty. 'Shit. Too late.'

'Hanna' springs like a cat, 'Hard' . . .

THWACK!

Kicks 'The Killer's' knee out at and odd angle.
Connects a hook. An elbow to the sternum.

A dive-bomb crosscut, sends 'The Killer'
sprawling to the ground. . .

All in a blur of movement.

Sickening efficiency.

'Hanna' silently slides a knife under. . .
'The Killer's' chin. . .
And slices it across his neck. . .

In his 'End', 'The Killer' is dying, while
regurgitating and gasping on his own blood.

Chapter 8

The Professor's Mystery

A MASSIVE SHANGHAI – CEMETERY: The weather is amazingly warm. A fresh breeze from the ocean sways the trees. We stay far.

Meifeng stands amongst a clump of PROFESSORS. A Buddhist priest recites the burial rites.
Bohai stands apart on his own.

LATER -- THE PROFESSORS HOUSE – SHANGHAI: Meifeng is in a cove of stacked periodicals and documents.

Her face is a little bruised from the car attack incident.
Shelves of books. Mountains of boxes already packed. A lifetime worth of knickknacks. By a man obsessed with history. All this chaos is overwhelming. She doesn't know where to start.

Mariner's instruments. Sextets. Astrolabe. Ancient charts. Paintings.
One of them a ship on land. Trapped in a sand dune.

Bohai walks in. Hangs back. Watches Meifeng as she reminisces. . .

"I've spent nearly all of my childhood in this room. Listening to him rehearse his lectures. Hiding under the piano as he played Chopin, badly.

It was the sea that really made him come alive.

Its treasures. Its secret. It's one
of the reasons Dad liked you so much: you
went after the secrets and treasures he never
could. . .

You also fought for revenge on the untold
horrors your family experienced under
Japan's rule."

Bohai pauses at a painting. A Greek figure
pulling up an attractive woman through the
depths of an abyss.

Meifeng continues softly. . .

"That's Orpheus's attempt to retrieve his wife,
Eurydice, from the underworld. . .

The University has already agreed to take all
of his papers, his research. . . I think. . ."

She doesn't finish. Probably hates herself for
the betrayal of drawing a line under her
Father's life work. . .as she adds. . .

"All Junk. A lifetime worth of obsessions."

One of his Professor friends, Professor
YINGJIE, pops his head around the corner.
A drink in hand, as he annotates her. . .

"Many ghosts in this room, Meifeng."

Yingjie's mouth, gaps wide-open as. . .

"Good GAWD Bohai, what happened to your
face?"

"A doorknob, Professor!"

"Fib a Chinaman. . .
Oh, the faculty has just arrived."

Meifeng reacts. . .

"Be right there, Professor Yingjie."

IN THE LIVING ROOM: Professor Yingjie
begins addressing the faculty. . .

"Phlebas the Phoenician, a fortnight
dead, forgot the cry of gulls, and the deep seas
swell and the profit and loss. A current under
sea picked his bones in whispers…"

We pull away from the scene…to find Meifeng,
Listening from the back wall. . .
A heavy heart. She walks out of the room.

AFTER THE EULOGIES: We drift through. The
men mingle. Swapping war stories.
They're at an age where funerals are
happening more frequently. We catch Bohai,
cornered by Professor Yingjie, regaling him
about the good old days…

"The Professor always said that Ninety-
Percent of Archaeology was done…"

Bohai finishes his thought. . .
". . .Was done in the library."

"Did you ever find that Destroyer, Bohai?"

Bohai squirms, as Yingjie carries on. . .

"No worries.

The Professor spent his life, scouring our coasts up into Korea and Japan and never found them.

He was obsessed with their stash, 'The Dragon Gold'.
Kept two diaries. One he used every day and a hidden diary."

"Well, you know...wait a minute..., Professor!"

"There's no shame in it, Bohai."

"Professor, Wait a minute. . ."

"Those 'Destroyer's' are just not here. The war thrived on misinformation.
Counterintelligence. Double bluff.
That sort of thing.
The charts were all wrong, Bohai."

"Professor, did you say, a 'Hidden Diary'?"

"Oh no, Bohai. I know that look. . .
That crazy, 'I'm going to jump off a building' look. I've seen it before; it never ends well."

"The 'Hidden Diary', Professor. . ."

Professor Yingjie cringes. He's said too much. Time to bail.

"Where is it?"

"It doesn't exist, Bohai. . .
Oh look, I need another drink."

Professor Yingjie scampers away, towards the home-made bar in the Living Room.

THE PROFESSOR'S STUDY: Bohai marches into the study. Energized with the possibility of finding the 'Hidden Diary'.

Tentative at first, then growing bold, he rummages in boxes.
Shifting stacks of magazines.
Looking through shelves.
Then he steps back for a panoramic view of the entire library.
His intuition kicking in . . .
Eyes scrutinizing the leather-bound bindings.
Then, an 'ah-ha moment'. . .

Moby Dick. 'First Edition' under glass. . .
He lifts the box.
Snaps the book off the pedestal. . .
And as he flips open the cover, sees a name. . .

"Gerhardt Braun?"

Suddenly, Meifeng comments from across the room, while he's lifting the Novel!

"It's a First Edition."

He lifts the 'Hidden Diary' from a hollow cavity inside MOBY DICK and begins reading. In moments, a second sense hits him as. . .

His head snaps around finding Meifeng looking over his shoulder.

She's staring at him, then the Diary. Confused. Then shock. Then fascinated, she speaks. . .

"Crap, Father kept another 'Diary'!"

Then pure 'fury flashes' across her face.

"You just couldn't wait, COULD YOU!

You've always been on this obsessive quest!
Your Family's lost legacy. The Dragon Gold!"

"It's not what you think, Meifeng. . ."

"Here? Now! Unbelievable."

She snaps the Diary out of his hand.

"Meifeng. . . just. . . just understand me. My
greater Quest, was GOLD on your finger
again."

"Get Out! NOW, Bohai!"

Everyone in the next room falls silent.
Professor Yingjie appears at the door.

Between Meifeng and Professor Yingjie's
disapproving stare, Bohai has no other choice,
but to actually leave.
He walks out.

She throws the 'Diary' on the sofa, as his
words start to sink in . . .
Then hating herself, she turns and runs after
him. . .

OUTSIDE THE PROFESSOR'S HOUSE: Bohai
weaves through the parked cars to get to the
street, when Meifeng comes running out the
house. . .

"Bohai. . . Bohai!"

Bohai stops and turns back momentarily. . .

"Look. . . I've had enough abuse for one day.
You're right. I'm a creep. I wasn't thinking."

Bohai falls sad. . .
Lost in a moment of self-realization. . .

"Maybe it's the funeral, maybe it's the booze.
Is this how I was, during our relationship?"

"I overreacted, Bohai. . .
Please, Come back in!"

"I don't know, Meifeng. . . It's. . ."

"Bohai. . . just come back in, please."

Instantaneously, their world grinds to a halt
as . . .
WHAAAM. . .

An incredible 'Fireball' consumes the
'Professor's House'. Splitting it into a
Thousand matchsticks.
Smoke and flames rising in the air! A roiling
pillar of fire. . .

The 'Concussion' knocks Bohai and Meifeng,
clean off their feet. Debris rains down --
floating ash and charred scrap.

Bohai and Meifeng scrape themselves up.
Shell-shocked. . .
'The House' is No More! A smoldering crater
in the middle of a posh neighborhood.
Only 'God' knows how many are dead?
This idyllic day has suddenly turned into a
'Nightmare'. . .

OUTSIDE THE REMAINS OF 'THE PROFESSOR'S HOUSE':   It's late evening, with local Neighbors milling around the front lawn. Gossip is rife.
Firemen still rummage around the smoking wreckage. The Coroners Van and two Black Hearses are parked nearby, waiting.

A FORENSIC TECHNICIAN is turning a piece of metal plate over with a flashlight and wire in her hand. . .
As expected, we find Detective Yuan, interviewing Bohai and Meifeng. Both of them staring off into the 'SKY' in traumatic stress-shock. . .

"Trouble seems to follow you two, Everywhere!"

Humbled by the catastrophic events, Bohai begins to think an answer for Yuan. . .

"We don't know who did this, if that's what you're asking."

Yuan turns his evil eye to Meifeng, who seems wrathful. . .

"You must have some kind of clue...What is it? . . . Is this kind of carnage, normal in your line of work?"

Meifeng seethes her answer softly. . .

"Come on. . .
You don't seriously suggest we've got something to do with this 'Horror'!"

"Your father's murdered a week ago. Now,
Today, you TWO walk out of his 'House',
precipitously only 'a minute' before it
disintegrates into ashes. . .
One of a coincidence, Huh?"

Meifeng's anger evaporates. Her argument
collapses, as she concedes the point to
Detective Yuan. . .

"I agree, this whole thing's pretty messed up."

Without an introduction. . . Yaun's 'Forensic
Tech' marches over with a charred, wired
gizmo in her hand. Detective Yuan takes her
aside and listens. . .

"Military. Foreign. Specialized. Very likely,
East German - Post War vintage."

Shocked, Detective Yuan repeats her words. . .
"East German - Post WWII?"

"Yup, 'Boss Man'! You read about this stuff,
but you never think you'll actually find one."

Detective Yuan 'Nods'. . . 'Thanks.'

Turns to Bohai, first -- searches Bohai's face,
for any betrayal sign. . .

"I better not discover you've got some 'Exotic
Hobbies', Son."

He stares a long moment at Bohai. . .Then
Meifeng. . .
Then relents, with his 'Nod', indicating. . .
'You TWO can Go'. . .

THE HAPPINESS NURSING HOME: Well appointed. Dotted with a few palm trees and local fauna. Manicured lawns.
A typical, Government Run, 'Old Folks Home' on the outskirts of Shanghai.
The old, the infirmed, and the forgotten haunt these corridors like ghosts.

Meifeng and Bohai walk in, 'Hot' on the back of another argument. . .as she adds. . .

"What makes you think he's going to help?"

"I saw his name, briefly in your Dad's 'Diary'. Besides, he's a foreigner, displaced in China since the Second World War."

Meifeng looks around the place. . .

"I don't think this man can even remember his name. Besides, how does he conceivably know 'German', if he's considered a 'Local'?"

"He's not a 'Local'. . .
His 'German Tender' sank here in 1945.
He spent Three years as a prisoner of war. Got married to a 'Local Girl'. Never went back to Germany. Taught German for Forty years at the grammar school. . .
I think he could use the distraction. . .
Don't you?"

"DID You, read all that in Dad's 'Diary'?
How long were you in his office, you creep?"

A NURSE breaks up the fight as she marches toward them. . .

"Sorry about the wait. Visiting hours are between. . ."

Bohai jumps in . . .

"We have an appointment. Mr. Braun?"

"Ah, yes. This way, I'm 'Nurse Ling'."

Without waiting, she marches off. Bohai and Meifeng quickly follow. . .

"You're the MAN from the 'News-Paper'. Meifeng 'chokes' out loud, then fires another charged look at Bohai. . . 'You lied, Again!'

She hisses a whisper. . .

"This is our marriage!?"

Bohai frowns: 'WHAT? I didn't have a choice.'

"I think it's Great that the 'Local Press' is taking an interest in him. . .

"Mr. Braun was my German teacher at School, 'Nurse Ling'."

Meifeng's shoots him another 'fiery' look. . .

"Idiot. You can't help yourself. . .
It's like 'Tourette's Syndrome'."

"At least, I didn't step out of our 'Marriage'."

"What does that have to do with anything? And we weren't together, when I met Zian."

"Arrrgh, the 'dial tone' now has a name."

"Not a 'dial tone'. He's just very. . ."

"What?"

"Not YOU! Honesty is his best quality."

She really wants to punch him right now. . .
All of this is going on behind 'Nurse Ling' as
she continues her banter. . .

"Any ONE here, could tell you an amazing
story. However, you didn't pick the chattier
patients. . .

"No?"

"Nope. Mr. Braun hasn't spoken in Ten years.
Since his wife died. . ."

Meifeng again shakes her head at Bohai: 'That
Figures, You Moron'. . .

"Pretty interesting life, though. He was a
German Tender Commander. Captured and
sunk right off 'Lingshan Island' at wars end."

This catches Bohai by surprise. . .

"Don't you mean, Qingdao Bay?"

"No. I'm not sure. I always mix up locations. I
can refer you to another patient. Mrs. Chen.
She's Ninety-Five.
She hasn't stop talking since '1987'."

They stop at the entrance of the
'Entertainment Room' as 'Nurse Ling' finishes
her 'Tour Guide' commentary.

"I'll leave you to it. But whatever you do, don't mention the WAR."

'Nurse Ling' smiles back as she walks away.

THE ENTERTAINMENT ROOM: This is where they host mahjong nights or big band dancing evenings.

Bohai's target, 'The Old Man', sits in a wheelchair. A blanket covers his legs and hands. He's staring out the bay windows, Towards the Sea.

Meifeng and Bohai approach him, as Bohai begins the introductions. . .

"Mr. Braun?"

No reaction.

"Mr. Braun. I'm here from the China Daily Courier Newspaper."

Meifeng rolls her eyes.

"I'm ah, I'm here to ask you a few questions."

No reaction. This is difficult. 'There must be a way in, a Key Word?'

"We made a discovery yesterday that might be of interest to YOU."

Mr. Braun's eyes remain lost. Fixed into nothingness.

Change of tactic. Bohai produces a photograph of the 'RING', now polished and resting in a velvet box. He levels it with Mr. Braun's eyes.

"Can you tell me what this 'German' inscription on the 'RING' says?"

Mr. Braun, remains 'Motionless' like a mannequin.
Then suddenly, his eyes flicker. Land on the 'RING'. A spark of life unexpectedly burns behind the irises.

Meifeng and Bohai exchange quick hopeful glances. . .
Bohai flips to another photo, a closer shot of the 'RING'. Exposing the inscription details inside the rim.

"Do these markings mean anything to you?"

The thrill in Mr. Braun's eyes is suddenly replaced by a scowl.
A haunted whisper escapes his lips. . .

"What?"

Braun spews it out. viciously. . .

"Ich schwöre bei gott diesen heiligen eid, daß ich dem Führer des Deutschen Reiches. . ."

Meifeng reacts, first!

"What's he saying?"

Suddenly, building into a torrent of German, a whirlwind of hateful diatribe flows forth.

". . .Und volkes Adolf Hitler, dem oberbefehlshaber der Wehrmacht. . ."

His mouth is now spitting out the words. Growing in amplitude, more hateful, sucking the air out of the room. . .

"Bohai? . . . Calm him down!"

"Unbedingten gehorsam leisten und als tapferer soldat bereit sein will. . ."

Meifeng and Bohai are pushed back by it. Confused as 'Idiot Pigs'. . .

At once, Mr. Braun spins the wheelchair toward them BOTH. Eyes blazing with a fury that energies him.

"Jederzeit für diesen eid mein leben einzusetzen. . ."

Then, Braun whips his blanket OFF his lap and jabs a crisp 'Heil Hitler' into the air.

It sends a jolt of fear through Bohai and Meifeng as they watch. . .Out of Control!

It's Mr. Braun's amputated wrist, that SHOCKS them. . .
Held firm in his Nazi salute. It's Chilling!

PARKING LOT OF THE NURSING HOME:
Visibly shaken.
Meifeng and Bohai are leaning against his Red
Toyota
As Meifeng tries to make sense of what
happened. . .

"I just don't understand how that deteriorated
in there, Bohai."

"These things run deep."

"Was it 'HIS HAND' that you found?"

"NO! No, I'm certain! I don't think so. Braun
was a German Tender Commander.
His boat sank off these parts, but. . . I . . . I just
don't know?!. . ."

"Do you know anybody else who speaks
German fluently?"

Thinking. . . they share a goofy smile. It's just
like old times again. And then the moment's
gone. Bohai comes to a silent decision and
heads back toward the 'Nursing Home'.

"What are you doing, Bohai?"

"Getting some answers. . ."

BACK INSIDE THE NURSING HOME: Bohai
zigzags around patients and old people in the
hallway.
He nearly collides with a man guiding an
elderly lady on her mobile bed frame.
He rushes back to the Entertainment Room to
again find Mr. Braun sitting in his chair, in
front of the Bay window.

Bohai braces himself for another confrontation.
Walks over. And 'DISCOVERS'. . .

Three bullet holes. One in the head. Two in the chest.
Head kicked back. Slack expression. Eyes dull.

It 'Knocks the Guts' out of Bohai!

He jumps back gasping for air. . .
The room is spinning 'Out of Control'.
A 'Sudden Realization' hits him, like a 'Ton of Bricks' as he SHOUTS. . .

"Meifeng!"

Instantly, Bohai 'zigzags' rushing around patients. Struggling to remain calm.
Heart rate pounding at Two-Hundred BPM. . .
Blood Pressure – Two-Fifty over One-Ninety.

Someone suddenly screams at the end of the hallway.
Panic grips him when Bohai sees Meifeng being forced into a Blacked-Out 'Landrover'.

Bohai RUSHES through the doorway, just as orderlies run in. Missing the Landrover by an inch, but Catching Meifeng's terrified expression against the rear window glass.

He runs to his Toyota. Two flat tires. Damn.
'Uh-oh.' Two orderlies run out of the Nursing Home.
Pointing him out. One is already on a Cell Phone. No doubt calling the Police.
Bohai. Runs. Like. Hell. Weaving through parked cars.

Sirens wailing in the distance. Trying to keep his eye on the 'Landrover', now vanishing into midday traffic. All hope seeps out of him when suddenly. . .
The Landrover veers left, then right, losing control, then. . .
WHACK. . .
Crashes into a telephone pole.

New hope. Bohai legs it. Sees Meifeng stagger out of the wreck. Dazed, battered, shaken. Somehow manages to lock eyes with Bohai rushing towards her through parked cars.

A Three Lane Highway separates them. . .
Meifeng is on the other side. Bohai trying to engage himself to run through traffic. Then he sees it. Right behind Meifeng.
'Hanna's' Operative. A mad freak. Marching towards her. Pistol grip in his fist. A 'Snipers Stare', locked on to Meifeng.

Bohai comes unglued shouting. . .

"Meifeng! Meifeng!"

But she can't hear him over the intense 'din of traffic'. Bohai's waving at her. Pointing behind her. Running toward her. . .

She doesn't understand. But her 'Sixth Sense' kicks in, as she spins to find -- His Pistol raised right into her face.
Finger locked over the trigger. Dead drop.

Trapped between heavy traffic and a bullet, Meifeng runs blind straight into oncoming traffic. . .

The sounds of squealing tires, bumpers smashing, drivers white-knuckle gripping of steering wheels as . . .
Bohai catches his breath, stunned.

All he could do is watch Meifeng lurch through the blue smoke of burning rubber.

Even 'Hanna's Operative' is momentarily taken aback by this. But insanely, he decides to plunge ahead through traffic, just as traffic resumes. Then changes his mind and decides the better of it and hangs back. Having lost his prey. At least for now. . .

AT NEARBY PEOPLES PARK: Filled with kids and moms. Meifeng and Bohai crouch into a tubular play module, as a short-term hiding place. . .

"Are you out of your mind?
Don't you ever look both ways?"

"Like I had a choice!"

"Is that the kind of responsible behavior you want for our kids?"

"Our kids? Our kids!
Hah! You don't want kids, Bohai. . ."

"It was ONLY, a hypothetical."

"So I'm getting crap, on your hypotheticals?
I was kidnapped, nearly shot, and run over!"

Bohai falls silent. His mind racing. His emotions are all over the place. We even catch a glimpse, a moment, between them: 'He's happy she's alive!' But that's wiped away fast.

"Who was that Guy?"

"The German Guy's, dead."

"You mean, Dead. . . DEAD?

Bohai's haunted look confirms it.

"Was he a friend of yours, Bohai?"

"What? Who?"

"The Guy with the 'BIG' Gun. . ."

"What? Are you out of your mind, Meifeng?"

"You're trying to get me bumped off, to get the other half of the house. . ."

"And of course 'The Boat'."

"That Boat's Mine!"

"Not after I get you, 'Bumped Off'. . ."

Bohai's attempt at a joke, sinks like lead.

"Who knows. You'll hitch yourself to any smuggler, thief, bandit with a 'Boat'."

"This is not my fault, Meifeng. . . See,
This is what always happens, when something goes wrong. . .
You always blame me!"

"This IS your fault. Everything goes wrong around you, this always happens! It's your obsession to revenge your 'Family's Legacy'!

They suddenly stop. Sensing someone else is there. A fat kid, eating a sloppy ice cream. He's been watching them intently. . . then smartly says. . .

"This is a Kid's area. Grow up."

Bohai cuts back at him. . .

"You're adopted, aren't you?!"

At that, the kid runs away, crying.

Meifeng nails Bohai with her evil eye. . .as he reacts. . .

"What?"

She changes the subject. . .

"That Guy!"

"What Guy, Meifeng?"

"Stop interrupting . . .the kidnapper 'GUY'! He was intent on killing me. . . But he needed answers first."

"This whole thing is out of hand!"

Maybe through instinct, habit, or new-found affection, Bohai stretches the sleeve of his shirt and dapples Meifeng's bleeding forehead. . .she continues. . .

"There was a woman in that Landrover, too. This is bigger than 'Treasure Scalpers', Bohai. This is a cover-up. A fucking 'BIG' cover-up."

They actually seem to be making-up. . .
And it's all told through their eyes. . .
'Bohai's Sorry' for the past.
'Meifeng's Sorry' for the past.
Both are very 'Grateful' they've made it out of
this. . .

When, Bohai suddenly jumps.
Police officers are here. . . They're questioning
folks all around the park. Maybe that stupid
kid, too. . .

"We gotta go, Meifeng!"

"To Talk to the police!?"

"No! Not now. . .
They think we killed the 'Old German.'"

Bohai pulls Meifeng along. . .

"To clear up the misunderstanding, then."

"I don't know who's behind all of this, but
something 'Dangerous' is going down. . ."

They both creep silently away. . .he whispers.

"And I can smell 'Treasure', too. And if there's
'Treasure' out there, I 'Can't Hunt' for it, from
inside a 'Prison Cell'."

"Then, there is only one man I know, who can
decipher this 'Mess', Bohai."

"Oh no. Oh No you don't! Not him..."

They vanish inside a Grove of Pagoda Trees. . .
Just as Police Detective Yuan approaches two
police officers in the Park.

"We've got an ID?"

He hands the ranking 'First Officer', a
mugshot of Bohai. . . He reacts. . .

"That's him! We found his car at the 'Nursing
Home'."

Detective Yuan sweeps his eyes across the
Park. And there, in the far corner, he catches
the last glimpse of Bohai and Meifeng. . .
Disappearing into rough terrain. . . Acacia,
Silk and Pagoda Trees. . .

Chapter 9

Uncle Longwei

A CHINESE SPECIAL FORCES CENTER - SHANDONG MOUNTAINS: Reserve Commander, GUI LONGWEI, shakes hands with some other Officers, then marches this way.
Big. Six-Foot-Six. Fifties. Shaved head. Looks like he could still force-march Fifty-Miles through hostile territory, on one breath.
Deep set eyes that are always searching, always scrutinizing.
Ex-Special Forces. He was born in Cammo gear for life.

We scan back to a makeshift camp entrance to see Bohai and Meifeng. They're waiting for him.

"Let me handle this, Bohai. He's my Uncle."

"I'm okay with that, for sure. He loves me."

"You're too blunt."

"He's a Soldier. He can handle it."

"Just, let me. . ."

Walking up on them, Longwei's big smile drops, seeing Bohai with Meifeng. Both are leaning against a picnic table.

He kisses Meifeng on her cheek. Smudging his black Cammo grease on her cheek.

"My Little, Meifeng!"

Bohai extends a hand, as Longwei wipes his Cammo colored hand on Bohai's shirt. Bad blood here.

"Unexpected. You guys aren't. . ."

"Together, Again? No . . . No, we're Not!"

"Relief. What can I do you for?"

Meifeng's just about to talk. . .when Bohai jumps in, first. . .

"We have a map. . ."

Longwei's eyes turn BLACK with HATE . . .

"Good for you."

Longwei walks off.

Meifeng fires a look at Bohai. . .'Told you to shut up around him'.

Both chase him about half a kilometer down the road from the Special Forces Center, below Mount Tai, to 'Longwei's Townhouse'.

Meifeng scolds Bohai the entire distance. . .

"He hates everything about YOU!
Meeting me. For asking me to Marry you.
For leaving me."

"I didn't leave you. You ran away."

"Don't say a word. He's the ONLY help we've
got left."

"I know that.
Don't you think, I don't know that?"

"Then 'SHUT UP!'"

ENTERING THE TOWNHOUSE: Once inside
Longwei's place, we see a wide open floorplan.
Clean and precise like the man himself.
Military pictures on the walls. Past services.
Africa, Southeast Asia, Iraq, various conflict
zones around the world. Group pictures. Most
of these men are now dead. Ghosts of old
friends.

Longwei's live in girlfriend DAIYU TING meets
them. Bohai can't help but share a
conspiratorial whisper with Meifeng.

"He's upgraded to a younger model, I like
that."

Meifeng responds sarcastically. . .

"Definitely something, I should look
into, as well."

Boom! 'Backfired'.
Bohai doesn't like that, at all. . .

Longwei motions Daiyu to bring drinks as he
opens up. . .

"Show me the 'RING'."

Bohai's Shocked. . .

"How did you know...?"

He lifts his hand to Bohai. . . 'Don't talk'.

Meifeng scowls at him! 'Just Shut Up.'

Longwei elaborates. . .

"Nothing else in 'Qingdao' gets you two more excited then. . .
The quest for 'Dragon Gold Treasure'.

Especially you Bohai, since your family got looted by the Japanese Empire!"

Bohai looks down. It's what has always eaten away at him, as he 'finally extends his arm out' to hand the 'RING' over to the Big Man . . . clearly scared to get too close to him.

Longwei pulls out a magnifying glass. Checks its detail. Expressionless. Methodical. Focusing on the inside bevel.

Bohai and Meifeng exchange worried looks.

"Where did you find this?"

Bohai desperately wants to talk. Meifeng signals: 'Don't'.

"Is it authentic, Uncle?"

Longwei pulls a 'Black Diary' out of a nearby desk. Then, a small reaction. Ready to reveal something. Preferably to, Meifeng ONLY!

"In the War, your Great Uncle Shen had
contacts in Japan and Korea and up in
Qingdao. Plus, agents for Japan as well as the
British.
They called them 'Doubles'."

"Great Uncle Shen was a 'Double Agent'??"

Bohai can't hold back. . .

"No. 'The Doubles', WERE Doubles."

Longwei and Meifeng fire looks at him.

Patience running out. Longwei flips the Diary
to a date entry. Then shuts the Diary –
He knows it by heart. . .

"In August. 1945 . . .Uncle Shen's Diary tells of
Prince Nakahito's last ditch effort to plunder
Gold out of China. . .

Bohai can't help himself, his mind is on fire as
he jumps in again . . .
"That was some of the looted 'Gold Heirlooms
and Jewels' my family lost. Those 'Empire'
Bastards."

And something amusing happens here: Bohai,
Meifeng, and Longwei begin to work in
tandem. . . as Meifeng enters the fray. . .

"There's more!
They wanted to resurrect 'Japan' financially
somewhere South, maybe the Philippines
where 'General Yamashita's' cave vaults were
located. . .

But, America got there first."

Bohai then adds his notes. . .

"Right. They're bastards, too. MacArthur sanctioned Hirohito's actions and took a massive amount of loot for himself!"

Longwei, again follows up. . .

"In '43, their plan was to build 'Custom Transport Destroyers'
The Kaba Class. . .
They were Modified to hold the entire inventories of untraceable processed 'Gold Bullion Bars' in their hulls, once they got to a forging plant."

Meifeng finishes his thought. . .

"The problem was to get to a safe port and processing forge quickly. Somewhere near China's shores."

Then Bohai adds. . .
"But Japan surrendered too quickly and the Destroyers were scuttled at sea with all their loot on board."

Meifeng continues. . .
"They never made it back to Japan."

Longwei finishes the follow-up. . .
"The diary holds the names of every
Officer and Boat that was assigned.
And the Officers initials were etched into each Imperial 'RING'.
They've never been found, 'til now."

He holds up the photograph of the 'RING'. The entire room converges to this one point.

Meifeng is drawn to it. It's like finding
Shangri-La . . .

"That's a good thing, Right Uncle?"

Daiyu returns with appetizers and drinks.
Bohai exchanges a tiny, but flirty smile with
her that Meifeng catches.
She pulls a face on Bohai, like she has 'just
vomited in her mouth'.

"It's Good and It's Bad. . .

The Good is: we now have an idea that the
Destroyer sank near Qingdao Bay.

Longwei looks at them BOTH . . .
"But where? And was there a forging plant
nearby?"

Bohai adds his historical knowledge . . .

"Most likely at Dadong Dao Island!? Recent
finds unearthed there suggest an underground
plant of sorts in a hillside.
The Destroyer could be at the Abyss."

Meifeng lights up at the challenge. . .

"It's a dangerous area of currents and
hazardous winds out there. . .
And just beyond its cliffs: Shipwreck Alley.
So . . . what's the Bad News, Uncle?"

"Other people have made copies of the
'Imperial Diary' with the initials of those
Officers, just like us."

Bohai finally, gets back in . . .
"So we've got competition."

"Who, Uncle?"

"I have a feeling we'll soon find out. . ."

Meifeng and Bohai exchange a look.

"They've probably got you tailed on every move. We've got to get you BOTH to a 'Safe Location' -- Tonight!"

Chapter 10

The Safe House

OUTSIDE THE TOWNHOUSE: Longwei's townhouse is not easy to find. It's hidden deep amongst Pagoda and Scrub trees.

One of Longwei's Security Team Operatives stands watch over the hidden location.

Then it happens. . . so fast it's hard for us to comprehend.
A knife flashes in the moonless night.
Across his throat, as a black hand mutes the scream. The limp body is dragged into the underbrush.

Bohai and Meifeng are loading their things into two Black SUVs, when Bohai gets a funny feeling. He scans the dark around them. Meifeng notices his concern. . .

"Bohai. What's wrong?"

The answer comes in a flurry of woodchips.

PPRRAAAAATTTT --
Bullets chew up the facade of the townhouse. Driving Bohai and Meifeng face first into the ground. Woodchips rain down on them like dandruff.

Longwei ducks out of the doorway -- another strafing stitches bullets in a zigzag pattern where he was standing.

Through clenched teeth, Longwei yells to Bohai . . .

"Where's the shooter?"

"I don't know, Colonel!"

Another volley whistles overhead. Meifeng freezes in an all-consuming, nano-second of panic.

ZING-ZING!
Shots WHIZ past. Shattering the SUV window near her.
Rounds smack the metal vehicle surface.

TINK-TINK-TINK!
Stitching quarter-sized holes.

And 'ah-ha'. Bohai sees it.
At the same time as Longwei does. Muzzle flash.
By the edge of the road. The shooter.

Longwei crawls under the SUV. Claws for his stashed automatic. Whips a couple of warning shots in the direction of the shooter.

The reply is swift. The SUV beside Bohai almost disintegrates under a spray of silenced sub machine-gun fire.

Within the Scrub Forest, 'The Shooter' slaps in a new clip. Aims and suddenly. . .

THACK!
Longwei's bullet explodes inches from 'The Shooter's' head.
Searching the townhouse for targets. . .
'The Shooter' drops his gun. Pulls out a knife.

Then melts into the foliage.

At the Townhouse parking area, Longwei halts his own movement. . .

"Did you see that, Bohai?"

"See what?"

"They stopped shooting and moved off".

"Two shooters, Colonel?"

"Maybe. Stay here..."

Tactical. He shoulders his automatic and creeps into the scrub brush. Invisible through the foliage. Suddenly spots 'The Shooter', who's also crawling through the brush. . .

Longwei cuts him down. He inches forward. And discovers. . .'The Shooter'. . . it's 'Hanna's Operative'.
Now punched through with multiple bullet wounds. Blood spattered on this face.
He's Wheezing. . .Longwei seethes at him. . .

"Who are you?"
Bohai and Meifeng also appear, just as he gurgles something indiscernible in his bloody last breath.
Finally accepting the end is near. . .

"Again. . . Who sent you?"

"He's a rogue agent, isn't he Colonel?"
'The Shooter' Operative smiles. Through the pain. At the absurdity of it all. His face a ghastly mask of blood. . .

Knowing he has given 'Hanna' time to escape...his eyes glaze over.
He's Dead.

Longwei, Meifeng and Bohai watch in stunned shock. . .
Longwei fingers the grass nearby. Blood.

"Blood. Someone else was here.
They're bleeding too. They can't be far away."

INSIDE A CHEAP ROOMING HOUSE: We creep through. . . the front door, it's partially left open.
Dark in here. A speckled trail of blood runs across the carpet. Black SWAT clothing strewn about.
We push toward a dagger of light coming from the . . . BATHROOM. . .

'Hanna' standing in only a bra and panties. Body bruised and mangled. Threading a needle through an angry cut across her rib cage. Wincing.
Biting down on the pain.
She braces herself. Knows this is going to hurt. She splashes sterile alcohol directly over the stitching. Then a blast of pain erupts as. . .

AAARRGGHH. . .

SHANGDON PROVINCE - THE COUNTRYSIDE NEAR MOUNT TAI: It's Late Night. A storm of birds spooks and takes to the sky in the partial starlight. . .
Longwei's surviving SUV rips through the narrow country road. In a white knuckle ride. Longwei shouts orders as . . .

"Daiyu, Let's double back to Matijiao. Map us to 'Jiang's Salvage Yard' near Qingdao Bay.

Longwei at the wheel giving orders. Daiyu navigating on the laptop.
Bohai and Meifeng in the back. Bracing against the pull of the road.

"Set up an exit and a 'Dive Boat', Daiyu."

Bohai and Meifeng eyes wide and tense. Daiyu. Fingers racing over keys. In her element. Wireless headset in her ear.

At the end of Lianing Road on an inner bay of the peninsular, Longwei shuts off the SUV's lights and glides into an alley beside some dilapidated docks, across from an oil refinery.

It's near, Matijiao Harbor, at a warehouse doorway. . .
When the silhouette of a MAN motions them to follow. The SUV disappears inside the massive metal doorway, as CLANG. . . they are sealed in.

Bohai and Meifeng, watch at the windows seeing people milling about. Mostly Military Types.
Men are talking near an inside dry dock --

An advanced tech YACHT about One-Hundred
Meters, is being loaded with supplies.
The SUV pulls up beside. . . an old Chinese
PLA Navy salt, Fifty-something.
It's Jiang, he greets everyone. . . starting with
Colonel Longwei.

"Ah, My Old Colonel! It's great to see you!

And you 'Both' as well, my young friends."

Longwei sweeps his eyes over the place. . .
'He's visibly very impressed.'

Bohai and Meifeng climb out of the SUV.
'Stunned'.
Clearly a villain's lair right out of a James
Bond movie.
Longwei's thoughts begin. . .

"Like the old days in the 'Gulf of Tonkin' with
the Yankees. Except this time, it's serious
'Unknown Operatives'.

"So who is it, chasing you, Colonel?"

"Don't know yet, Jiang. They're connected.
They have plenty of tech, muscle and money.
And they seem to be a step ahead of us. . .
Even found MY PLACE, deep in the 'Tai
Mountains'. . ."

He looks at Bohai and Meifeng. . .

"We've got to secure these Two, Now!
I've already lost a Man to these 'Animals'. . .
Then, we'll go salvage 'Secrets'. . .
In deep water. . .
Where can we talk, Jiang?"

"My office, Colonel."

Jiang turns to face Daiyu, pointing. . .

"Daiyu, take everyone to my 'Operations Room', over there, and get yourselves fortified. We'll be back shortly with a PLAN, I'm sure!"

Jiang leads the way up a side staircase into an office overlooking the dry-dock expanse. Longwei looks back at the beautiful lines on the streamlined high-tech yacht.

"That's one beautiful piece of equipment, Jiang. Who owns it?"

"It's 'Salvage', now. Bought it in Hong Kong from the Chinese Government. . . They seized it from a Ukrainian Oligarch . . .
I've had it a year now!"

Jiang moves in behind his desk. Pours two double whiskies at his back-bar.

"Got a 'RING', Jiang. . .
A Matsu Class Destroyer!
The KABA - 5505.
Found one possible Commander from my 'Diary'. . . 'Edo Ozawa'!"

Jiang hands a full whisky glass over to Longwei. Falls back into his chair. Silent, but Pondering.

"The legend. 'The Dragon Gold' loot, stolen by the 'Japs' from all the peoples of Shandong Province."

The Colonel continues. . .
"Poor 'Bohai's Entire Family', they were made into Japan's slave laborers. Once known as the richest landowners in Qingdao.
He's all that's left of them and their wealth. . .
And he has nothing himself, but the ambition to regain it!"

A slight flicker of interest from Jiang. He's listening, as he opens up too. . .

"There's some nasty people out there that wish that 'Dragon Gold Legend' would go away -- Japan's Bankers for 'Starters', since they stole it. . .
The Americans and the CIA since they screwed us ALL over at wars end and hid the facts on 'Yamashita's Gold Vaults' in the Philippines!

And then, 'More Likely' those 'World Banking Cartels' that now hold 'Chinese Gold' in their vaults, far away and unrecoverable in 'New York and Switzerland'. EVIL Greed!
Now they want more, too. . ."

Longwei gulps down his whiskey, as he simmers thinking, 'It's TRUE'. . .
That fact had occurred to him too and he feels it's also the MOST Likely. . . .as Jiang adds!

"Banking Cartels have always covered up where ACTUALLY, they got their massive 'Gold Assets' after WWII. . .
Nazi 'Holocaust Gold' in Switzerland pales at the volume of gold, jewels and artifacts looted from China and Southeast Asia. Even the Brits and Dutch Gold hoards in Hong Kong and Singapore, now sit in underground 'Cave Vaults' or offshore Banks like the Caymans!"

Longwei pulls out the photograph of the 'RING'. Presses it on Jiang's desk.

"Bohai and Meifeng were almost killed, several times in the last Forty-Eight-Hours! They'd discovered a rotted hand with the 'RING' on it. Now they're sure the KABA sank near here, not off Japan's shores."

"Where, exactly Colonel?"

"The Abyss probably. Just at the harbor entrance to 'Dadong Dao Islet'."

Dadong Dao Island

Jiang thinks about that. Can't help but be impressed with that conclusion. And a little concerned. . .

"Serious water my friend!
Two-Thousand Meters Deep. Maybe Three.
From cliff to bottom, there's no known shelf."

He fiddles with the photographs, then scrutinizes the initials in the 'Bevel' photo.

"Was this Officer physically on board?"

Longwei pulls a small stack of other photocopies from inside his leg pocket. Copies of the notorious 'Imperial Diary'.

"This ties the Commander to the 'RING'."

Longwei fishes in his pocket, tosses Jiang the actual Gold 'RING'.

"And that's the 'RING', Jiang! Authentic. Links it to 'The Dragon Gold'."

"We're talking a lot of equipment, Colonel. And that's going to draw attention. . . Official Government Agencies, Our PLA Coast Guard and most likely of all, those idiot Criminals, chasing the Gold Bullion."

Longwei walks to the window overlooking the vast Warehouse floor below.

"You've got one piece for us already; right here in dry-dock, Jiang."

Longwei grins. He could sell 'Shit to a Pig Farmer'. . .

QINGDAO AREA - THE SAFE HOUSE
Weapons. Handguns. Semi-automatics.
Knives. . .
Everything, packed into two army canvass
bags with equipment. All of it, now located at
the 'Safe House'.

We're in the downstairs living room of an old
'German Landhouse'. Nineteen Forties Era,
European design. Comfy. Overlooking the
entrance to Qingdao Bay.

Meifeng is on her laptop. She's scanning
through research.

Bohai starts fooling with his camera to check
out the photos from the original ROVER Dive,
as Longwei comes up to him. . .

"Mind if I see that HAND photo?"

Bohai yields Longwei the camera. . .
The Colonel concentrates on the photo screen.
Zooms, Zooms-in further. Then scans the arm
and the hand's leathery surface. He's silent.

"What do you see in his photos, Uncle?"

"I'm trying to understand the lack of
deterioration after Seventy-Years.
It has to be the Depth Effect. . .
The Temperatures. The Abyss Itself. . .

Its depth is unknown. Severe wind. Wave
turbulence. No one has ever dived this deep on
'Dadong Dao Island'."

Meifeng jumps in with her info. . .

"Dadong Dao Island and the area over the Abyss is actually a favorite spot we use for 'Kitesurfing'. . . Bohai uses it a lot!"

Bohai, then adds his feelings about it. . .

"And, for 'Romantically' inclined couples to hide away from prying eyes."

His obvious dig at Meifeng.
As, Meifeng continues without accepting his challenge. . .

"It can't be 'that' deep, Uncle?"

"I would guess, Meifeng, One to Two thousand Meters, right at the mouth of the Harbor entrance. . .

'Whoa Doggy!' That number travels the room as Longwei continues. . .

"The extreme 'Cold Water' clearly preserved it. At the Abyss, the first major thermocline starts at Three-Hundred meters, dropping the temp to below Forty degrees."

The Colonel looks back at Meifeng. . .

"Below Eight-Hundred Meters, it's subfreezing. . .
You can't dive that, without self-contained 'Atmospheric Suits' or at the very least a 'Deep Ocean Bathysphere'."

Now, he glances at Bohai. . .

"A Thousand-Meters Down, if the Destroyer's storage is intact, that would keep everything inside preserved, like canned tuna."

Finally, the Colonel stares at Bohai. . .

"Of course, if the ship's been damaged, things like your severed hand here, Bohai. . .
Could break out into open-water.

As for the Destroyer and the Gold, it just might sink into the Abyss, if it hasn't already. . ."

CHEAP ROOMING HOUSE: Organized and Laid-Out for action, are all kinds of weapons. Small arms, fully-automatic Rifles, Stilettos.

Area Maps and an 'Open Laptop' are in front of her. . . as Hanna's voice echoes through the room, but no one is there, just 'Hanna. . .
She's talking on-line, using her computer. . .

"They've re-positioned into a 'Safe-House' near the Naval Museum at Qingdao Bay."

VanBoveen's face, glows on her 'Laptop Screen'. . .
"Don't worry about that 'RING', now!
Stay in contact. Observe only. We need to find who they've employed to help them, and if they know which island to search, before we close in."

AS OUR VIEW SWEEPS THROUGH THE ROOM: Face down on the floor lies a DEAD Cleaning Lady. . .Two holes punched into her back, in each lung, a scarlet pool at her head. As we continue drifting through the shadowed Room, we again see 'Hanna' in her Black SWAT outfit. . .
The glow of the 'Laptop' giving her a ghostly pallor as 'The Voice' on the 'Laptop' continues.

"If you're discovered. . . use 'EXTREME' prejudice."

At once, the signal 'CUTS OUT'. Transmission OVER. . .

ROYAL DUTCH BANK - COUNTRY ESTATE - SHANGHAI: Cozy warm Fireplace burning. A well, appointed room with cathedral style windows overlooking a manicured green lawn.

We observe 'Mr. VanBoveen' as he closes his 'Laptop'. Snaps up his cell phone, then calls a high ranking Chinese Official, as he speaks in perfect 'Mandrian'.

"Get me the Commandant of the PLA Coast Guard, Admiral Hsu at his Home!"

NAVAL HEADQUARTERS: Qingdao. China

The call is routed through, to a groggy VOICE, just waking after a long Mission Day. Answering in 'Mandrian'. . .
"Admiral Hsu, Here . . ."

"It's 'VanBoveen' with 'Royal Dutch', Admiral. . . I'll need another small favor, per 'Our Special Agreement'. . ."

Chapter 11

The Dragon

QINGDAO BAY - EARLY MORNING:
There's a pre-dawn chill in the air, as an enormous steel door grinds open. . .
We see a sleek high-tech One-Hundred-Meter Superyacht glide past us, out of Jiang's salvage facility. . . on the stern, its name in Mandrian, *'The Dragon'*, stands out to us. . .

Crewmembers are on-board with QBZ-97 (5.56 mm) assault rifles. On alert for potential threats.
The yacht drifts quietly into the open bay then out into the Yellow Sea off Qingdao. Jiang, at the helm. Watching his team smoothly operate.

Darkness hides their movements as they leave the bay behind.
From the Bridge, Jiang has a smirk -- a feeling of absolute power.
Then. . . something pings on radar. A large BOAT moving up near them.

Jiang gives an order. . .
"We've picked up a visitor, BE ALERT!"

It's still dark as 'The Dragon' glides into the main channel out toward Dadong Dao Island. Fog is starting to enter the surrounding Bay.

The Crew has an ID' on a PLA Coast Guard Boat, gaining to their rear as. . .

The Yacht's Turbines Rev smooth and quietly. Hardly making any ripples in its wake. Maneuvering past dozens of large foreign Freighters and Oil tankers anchored in holding positions outside the main channel. . .

Jiang routes them quickly, into a hidden area North of the Shandong Peninsular.

On Board the approaching Peoples Liberation Army (PLA) Coast Guard (CG) Frigate, their Captain, scans the moored boats. He watches for any movement, but it's impossible for him to visually see through the mass of freighters and Oil Tankers anchored and moving in and outside of the Harbor, without helicopter support. . .

At that moment, the PLA CG Executive Officer (XO), gives a Radar Report to the Captain. . .
"We lost him, Sir."
The PLA CG Captain replies back. . .
"He'll be there. Somewhere."
The XO adds his request. . .
"Can we get 'HELO' support, Sir?"
"Too much fog for that, XO. We'll pick him up later. Besides, I know where he's going."

Jiang is monitoring his own Radar, as the PLA Coast Guard Frigate rushes its search and skims past the outer Harbor Buoy heading back in the opposite direction. . .

Jiang immediately engages the Yacht's Turbines to AHEAD FULL. . .

The High-Tech Superyacht smoothly cuts a wake out into open water.
The Powerful twin turbines effortlessly rev up, swirling the sea into a white foam, as the 'The Dragon' moves Northeast, cloaked by the Moonless Night. Then disappearing silently into the 'Black Waters' of the Yellow Sea.

THE SAFE HOUSE: It's Morning, but still dark outside. They're in the Master Suite. The only light in the room is the laptop screen glowing against Meifeng's soft features.
She watches Bohai. Asleep in the king-sized bed. A tinge of regret colors her cheeks. Like old times.
The laptop screen flashes masses of web information:
'General Yamashita Tomoyuki's' Gold Caves and Vaults for loot stolen from Southeast Asia, World Banking Cartels control of Dragon Gold, MacArthur and Hirohito's Agreement to cleanse Japan of any reparations for WWII, Citibank and the CIA, and finally Himmler's stolen Holocaust Gold, hidden in the Harz Mountains of Germany.

Bohai sees her light on. . .

"For a moment, I thought I was home."
He looks at Meifeng's beautiful face. He too has the same feeling. Her face looks so innocent as he inquires. . .

"Can't sleep?"

"I've found them, Bohai. The Banks. They're the 'Criminals'! They're the ones chasing us."

"The Banks, Meifeng?"

"Yes, YES! It's all about Looted Gold from Sovereign nations. If the news media finds out, every banking cartel in the world including the Americans and the CIA will want it hidden away forever to cover their crimes against China. . .
We have to find that 'Destroyer' before anyone else does."

Bohai drags himself up and beside her. Leans over. Watches a parade of images flash by. There's an intimacy here that they haven't felt for a long time.

She blinks, baffled by this man beside her.

She tries to squeeze out a smile. Then pulls away. She moves to the window. She needs to catch her breath.
It overlooks the dark and foreboding Yellow Sea. A warm orange smear of a new day is slowly breaking in the East. . .
See can see its faint edge, just as. . .

PFFT!
Something strange has happened.
A flower on the table breaks in half. By itself.
Weird.
Meifeng follows its imaginary trajectory to the bedroom window where a silver star marks an entry through the glass. At Meifeng's head height. . .

Suddenly she realizes as she turns. Bohai is down. Blood pouring from his shoulder.

"BOHAI!"
She tackles him to the floor just as hell
ERUPTS. . .
. . . PFFT-PFFT-PFFT
Silencer shots rip through the windows. . .
showers of shards are everywhere. Chewing
up furniture into kindling.

Meifeng falls over Bohai. Face to face. Shit
flying around them. She shoves and pushes
him to the doorway. They crawl, with him
bleeding, through a whirlwind of CHAOS.
Bullets riddle the air. . .
Instantly, Longwei is there, at their doorway
as he drags Bohai out.
Longwei
"THEY'RE HERE! OUTSIDE!"

"How Many, Uncle?"

"WE DON'T KNOW! GET OUT!"

Just as fast, the shooting stops. Woodchips,
fluff, and material drifts through the air like
snow.
When, something the size of a softball crashes
through the shattered glass. Hits the back wall
with a metallic thud.
Rolls into the hallway between them. Longwei
sees it. So does Meifeng. Bohai is dazed, as he
remarks . . .

"What is it?"

Longwei grabs Bohai and drags him
downstairs. . . as again bullets start 'barking
all around' them –

They rush like bats escaping …bullet hits blasting craters in the wall, chasing them down the stairs out the hallway. . .

They rip out the back door, pushing themselves to go faster, away from 'The Safe House'. . . when –

WHAAAAM
Half the house comes alive in a mushroom of magnesium light. Swelling walls out. Pulverizing the building, in a ball of fire. An angry black cloud boils into the sky.

The concussion scatters all 'THREE' of them flat against the ground.
Ash descends around them. Senses stunned. Disoriented.
They scrape themselves up.
As Longwei runs for the SUV. Meifeng drags Bohai to safety. . .
FINALLY, all in!
The Colonel peels the SUV out of there like a scalded jack-rabbit.

From an AERIAL VIEW. . . The SUV guns down the road.
While out front of the House remains, a TEAM IN BLACK invades the wreckage. Automatics shouldered. Sweeping for life.

Further OUT. . . Longwei is tearing down the road. Meifeng is screaming. . .

"UNCLE, UNCLE, WHERE'S DAIYU! We left Daiyu behind!"

Just then, Longwei slams on the breaks to a skidding halt.

Throws the passenger door open. . .
As Daiyu leaps in. Thumbs up.
Longwei stomps the accelerator.

Again they peel out, in a burst of gravel, as
Daiyu casually remarks. . .

"Got Three, Babe. They're Independents.
No tattoos.
No ID's, either."

Meifeng applies pressure to Bohai's shoulder
wound. . . and Daiyu tosses her the 'ER Kit'
from under the front seat!
Quickly, Meifeng places a dressing over
Bohai's wound, as she hollers. . .

"Damn, Girl! You're 'DEADLY' Dangerous."

Bohai's eyes roll back, as he . . .
"I'm really getting. . . DIZZ. . .EEY. . ."
. . . Passes out.

The SUV rips down a hidden back road.
Then, in moments, it disappears, lights out,
under cover of foliage, darkness and scrub
Pagoda Trees. . .

PART TWO

GOLD & TREASURE

Chapter 12

Hang's Bathysphere

HANG'S DIVE FACILITY: Within a harbor near the Olympic Sailing Center, lies Hang's operations. It's a scene right out of Ian Fleming's Thunderball, two small commercial bathyspheres, suspended by ceiling lifts over an internal seawater 'moon-pool' with under building access to the nearby Bay.

Guozhi Hang, a Fifty-something cigar smoking playboy and want-a-be professor, marches through his dive facility -- his techno toy kingdom, as Jiang, his erstwhile business associate, struggles to keep up. . .

"Last time I let you convince me to lease you one of my BEEBE's, it ended up costing me Seven-Grand USD in damages. . .

Jiang laughs sarcastically. . .
"That Guy's gone, Guozhi."

Jiang halts. Guozhi spins to face him, as he continues. . .

"Here's the deal.

Not only do we use your man, 'The Professor' to drive it, we pay for your 'Support Boat' to ferry it out to our coordinates."

Hang quickly remarks back. . .
"Up front, that's Ten-Thousand USD. One day. And you close the Official 'Sealed' Government paperwork yourself, to okay the job.
No PRC confiscations for errors either."

Hang grins at Jiang. . .
"You got that on you, Ole Boy?"

"Hang, it's a big salvage job, but the Money is already available. . .
Jiang produces a metal 'Briefcase'.
Guozhi halts, shakes his head, 'with caution on his mind', he opens the 'Briefcase'.

"I should know better than to go into business with you again, Jiang. But, damn it, I'm intrigued and Money is Money!

"Fifteen-Thousand US Dollars, to be exact, right there in your eyes, Hang! Your Ten, plus Five extra to cover your personal expenses. . .
Are we, back in Business?"

"Okay, Okay. . .Jiang. . .We're back in Business!"

Jiang shakes his hand and closes the 'Briefcase'.
"Here's the drop coordinates for 'The BEEBE'. I'll call you on the final 'GOTO' coordinates when we get in position. . .

If the current's too rough, we'll abort.
No refund -- you keep it all."

Guozhi takes up the 'Briefcase'. Weights the heft in his hands. Eyes Jiang carefully, as he speaks. . .

"I'm presuming this extra 'Five K' has something to do with the PLA Coast Guard.

They're 'Broadcasting' every hour, for everyone to stay clear of 'Dadong Dao Island' and that Zone, near the 'Blue Abyss'."

Jiang hangs a crooked smile. Won't reveal a thing.

"We'll need that 'BEEBE' with the remote hands this time. . . Not that 'toy' you rent out to rich tourists."

Guozhi matches Jiang's grin. He Likes the challenge, nods his 'Okay'!

"And, Guozhi, we could be down to Eight-Hundred Meters or so, depending on our target."

Guozhi loses his grin. Damn. Shit.

"And I want that Official PRC paperwork done too, Jiang. . . No excuses. . ."

Without looking back, Jiang quickly joins his Crew, as they board 'The Dragon' Superyacht.

Colonel Longwei arrives with his team, while Bohai nurses his shoulder and Meifeng unloads their gear into the stern storage area of the Superyacht, along with Daiyu, who has already loaded up her jet-boat into the storage area.

Finally, Longwei addresses Jiang. . .

"They found the 'Safe House' and started shooting.

We escaped unharmed, except for Bohai."

Jiang notices Bohai standing at the stern. . .

"How's he holding up?"

Longwei says nothing. For the first time, he really doesn't know, even about Meifeng's attitude either.

Both Bohai and Meifeng are still on the stern of the Superyacht talking. . .
Daiyu leaves them silently, as she makes her way up to the Bridge, joining the Colonel and Jiang.

Bohai seems very serious. Repentant, as he whispers to Meifeng. . .

"You know, Mei. . ."

"Don't call me that. . .anymore, Bohai!"

Undaunted, Bohai continues. . .

"If the last few days have taught me anything, it's this. . ."

"Don't say it. Don't open that wound, Bohai, not now. . ."

Still he continues. . .
"I may have not been the best friend you
wanted. . . I may have imposed my family on
you. . . my mother in our home. . ."

"Bohai, don't start this up, after all we've been
through, today."

"I may not have given you the attention you
wanted or needed, because I was too busy
clinging to the Old Ways. . . the Past. . . being
an Honored Husband. . ."

"Bohai, we're not getting back together. I can't
be ruled by your traditions from 'Old China'.
I'm my 'Own Woman' now!"

"Nearly loosing you back there. . . Twice,
Meifeng. . . taught me that I'd rather see you
Free and Happy, then miserable with me in a
traditional marriage."

Surprisingly, He produces the 'Divorce
Papers'. Hands them over to her. Then walks
off the Ship's Stern, onto the Dock. . .

Everyone on the Bridge, catches a glimpse of
Bohai. . .
As he climbs onto the Main Dock. . .he looks so
pitiful with his arm sling, not turning back.
Meifeng is stunned.
She flips through the Divorce Papers. . .
All of it, signed. She's won. . .
And somehow, as she watches him go away,
it's not a Victory at all. . .

Maybe she'll at least get him back on-board,
since they're going to need every last one of
them, to overcome this formidable enemy!

Chapter 13

Billions in Gold Bullion

ROYAL DEUTSCHE BANK - SHANGHAI:
In 'REAL-TIME. . .Vanboveen is staring at a
Large Multi-Frame 'Financial Projection
Screen'. . . in the 'Funds-Wire-Transfer Room',
deep in the compound building of RDB. . .
It's mid-afternoon.
A Bank Security Field Agent in SWAT gear
appears in one of the frames, as he speaks
directly into his laptop to Vanboveen. In the
frame's background, the 'Professor's House' is
still burning. . .

"No bodies in the wreckage, Sir."

Vanboveen orders him to report. . .

"And the 'Targets'?"

"Escaped, Sir.".

"Secure the scene. Then 'Clean-Up anything
incriminating. . .
You've got two hours."

VanBoveen adds a second 'LIVE' frame onto
the multi-frame monitor. . . as 'Hanna's Face'
appears. . .

"Don't fail me, Hanna. I want them 'Dead', but
wait 'til we know, where that 'Dive' is located!"

She smiles. The cruel smile of a shark about to
strike. . . Then her IMAGE 'BLINKS' OUT.

Financial transactions once again appear on all frames of the multiple image screen. Streaming numbers. . . in columns, from various worldwide accounts.

ROYAL DEUTSCHE BANK - HONG KONG: LATER
BURN UP: HONG KONG, CHINA
Another Secret 'Vault-Like-Transaction' Room within the bank complex.
Video monitors. Four frames with financial data streaming.
It's Chairman Haughton, and he's watching all screens. Letting nothing slip his attention as he directs orders to. . .
The Bank's Senior Clearing Clerk. . .

"What is our current System-Wide 'Gold Bullion Inventory', Suzi?"

"Sir, Forty-Thousand Troy-Ounces in Four-Hundred ounce, London Standard Bars. . .
At Today's SPOT: That's Two-Point-Six Billion US Dollars. . .

"Suzi. . . What would One-Thousand-Tons calculate to, in Ten-Kilogram Bars?"

The Clearing Clerk contains her audible 'GASP' of surprise as she comes back. . .

"Swiss, Sir?"

"No, roughly estimate it. . . in 'Generic Ten Kilo' Bars. . .

"Sir, that could create a massive 'Worldwide (T&R) Transfer and Reconciliation' prob . . .

"Just, Do It, Suzie. . ."

Crazy, she thinks . . . 'Okay Boss', as she jumps into number crunching time. Then the eye-popping answer appears directly on the Chairman's monitor. . .

"Sir, it's . . . 'Fifty-Five-Point-Three Billion' US Dollars."

Suddenly, ANOTHER FRAME on the MONITOR screen pops up, as . . . GANG ZHI is now on the line. . . Haughton remarks. . .

"Gang Zhi. . . A change of plan. . .
Contact your secret friend deep inside the PRC Documents Division. . .
And get us a back-dated 'Twenty-Year Oil and Gas Lease' for a Ten-Kilometer drilling zone off Dadong Dao Islet in the Yellow Sea off Qingdao. . .

Dadong Dao Oil Zone in the Yellow Sea

THE ABYSS - DADONG DAO ISLET:
The expanse of Ocean. . . it's like 'Melville's
Sea, from Horizon to Horizon.'
A tiny speck of advanced technology is drifting
on its shimmering glass surface. It's Jiang's
Superyacht, 'The Dragon'. . .

We visualize the colossal CLIFFWALLS on
Dadong Dao, set in the Yellow Sea, near
Shandong Province. . .
'The Dragon' is positioned over the 'Deep
Abyss' at Dadong Dao. . .

Colonel Longwei watches cautiously toward
the horizon. He's observing a nasty wall of
storm clouds moving in, with overcast and sea
swells building forward of the arriving Front.

Overhead, a Chinese PLA, 'Z-10 Fierce
Thunderbolt' Helicopter flies low in, over
them. . .

It is obviously meant to intimidate, as it lands on a CHINESE PLA FAST ATTACK FRIGATE. It's the Coast Guard's High Tech, 'YueyJang', and it's idling only Ten-Kilometers from Dadong Dao Island. . .

Jiang announces to his 'Dragon' Crew. . .
"We got company, folks."

'THE DRAGON' – BRIDGE: The Superyacht, sways with the growing Four-Foot swells. Several crewmembers on the bridge are working a battery of video screens and high tech instruments.
Bohai and Jiang prepare the DIVERS for a quick descent to the 'Abyss'.
Bohai speaks up first. . .
"It's my find. . . I should be doing this."

"It's too dangerous, Bohai."

Static breaks in on the radio, THEN. . .
A PLA COASTGUARD 'voice' breaks in . . .

"Superyacht 'DRAGON'. . . What are your intentions?"
Jiang immediately picks up. . .

"It's Captain, Jiang Zhee, on board 'The Dragon' Superyacht. . .
I'm hereby requesting to speak you're your 'Commander Liao'."

Silence. . .
In moments, another 'voice' comes over the radio. . .
"Captain, Jiang Zhee, it's 'Commander Liao'. How can we assist you, my 'Old Comrade'?"

"Commander Liao, it's my pleasure to hear your 'Voice' again after many months at Sea. . . . Hope all is well with You, Your wife and Your Family, Commander."

"Ah yes, we are well. Hope to hear you are also, Captain Jiang."

We need a favor Commander, we're on a 'Repair Test Run' of 'The Dragon's' updated engines and hull design in rough water and need some time to complete that."

The Commander replies somewhat officious.

"Jiang. . . 'The Admiral' has temporarily placed these waters in a 'Ten-Kilometer Restricted Zone'."

Damn. Jiang needs more time.
Gestures to his First Mate: ALL STOP.
Jiang comes back with a proviso. . .

"Will comply, Commander. However, we have a slight 'Vibration Problem' on our starboard propulsion jet. And I've had to 'shut down' engines!"

"Jiang, we can only allow Twenty-Minutes, or 'Under Sanction' we'll have to Board and Tow your vessel."

Damn. That's 'Not Enough Time'. Jiang tries to gain some ground. . .maybe a hidden ploy. . .

"That's good, Commander Liao, that's good! We'll Comply - OUT. . ."

THE ABYSS AT DADONG DAO ISLAND:
Four foot and higher swells are now battering
the sides of the Superyacht, 'DRAGON', as it
idles, while waiting to discharge the 'Divers'.

DIVE MOON-ROOM: The floor is opened to
release the DIVERS. They're suited up and
ready to go, as another even larger wave
hammers the ship and shakes everything loose
in the Moon-Room unexpectedly. . .

It causes a 'Rack' of OXYGEN CYLINDERS to
tumbledown onto both the 'Divers'. They're at
once pinned, as Jiang, Meifeng and Bohai rush
in. The 'Divers' start shouting. . .

"Roll the cylinders off."

Jiang shouts back nervously. . .

"Hai, speak to me!"

"I think I broke my arm, Jiang."

Bohai helps Diver #2, quickly testing him
visually. . .

"How many fingers do you see?"

Bohai makes a fist for DIVER #2. . .
"Three."

'Shit.' Bohai exchanges looks with Jiang.
'What now?' Then, in an impulse of pure
madness- Bohai states. . .
"I'm going, Jiang."

"You can't, Bohai."

Meifeng, then jumps in . . .

"Not without me."

Meifeng's face is dead set on going, as Jiang cautions her. . .

"You 'Guys' are nuts. Besides, Bohai has a shoulder wound."

"We're both experienced 'Divers', Jiang"

"No."

Bohai tries to rationalize with him. . .

"Time's running out, Jiang!"

"Then we abort."

Meifeng adds her opinion. . .

"We can do this. . .together!"

From the Moon-Room window, she points to the 'BEEBE Rover" hanging on davits, outside on the rear deck.

Arriving into the emergency and overhearing all this, Colonel Longwei pops into the fray. . .

"Absolutely NOT. My niece is not going anywhere near that thing."

BRIDGE - 'THE DRAGON' YACHT: They've all returned to the Command Bridge.
Bohai and Meifeng are sitting in chairs at the rear, restricted from leaving.
Spotting the CHINESE CG Frigate, Jiang lowers his binoculars.

"The Coast Guard's approaching. We're bailing."

Meifeng requests to be excused. . .

"Can I, at least, go to the toilet?"

Longwei motions: 'Yeah, sure.'

We catch it, a slight pause at the door, a slight tilt of her head, a signal to Bohai: 'Follow me.'

Bohai stands, as Longwei catches him. . .

"Where do you think you're going?"

"Below deck, Colonel. . . Might as well get this shoulder down. . .
I really need a Nap, since we're not needed up here."

Without objection, Bohai leaves too.

Through the 'Broadcast Speaker', the Radio lights up with the Coast Guard Commander.

"Jiang. We're coming on Board."

Longwei looks at Jiang for direction. . .
"What do we do now. . .!?"

Seeing something at the Stern, Guozhi Hang yells out to the crowd. . .

Those 'Young IDIOTS' are taking My 'ROVER'!

'What?' All heads spin, then rush out on the upper Deck to see. . .

Meifeng and Bohai, fighting against the spitting rain, are boarding the 'Rover' Bathysphere, as Jiang and Longwei explode off the Bridge down to the lower rear deck.

Fast as 'Hell', Bohai enters, then slips into the 'Command Seat'. Powers up the 'Rover's' computers, as Meifeng smiles to Jiang and Longwei, both rushing up to outside the 'Rover's Main Hatch.

Nearly there, she salutes them and . . .
SLAMS the 'Hatch' cover shut.
Sealed and Locked. . . she grips the Release Lever exchanging a quick look with Bohai. . .
YANKS IT . . . Then. . .

CLIIICK!
The Rover Releases from its rigging and FREEFALLS Ten-Meters into the 'Growling Sea Waves', tossing water that same distance back up to the Stern Deck. . .

SPLAASSH!
Jiang and Longwei watch 'Helplessly' frustrated, with total disbelief, as the freed 'Bathysphere' digs its way deeper into the vicious swells. Then disappears under the Black Ocean Waves.
Wind tossed, balancing against the deck, Longwei surrenders, a smile of admiration.

"Damn Plucky Girl."
The Colonel's grin says he: 'Liked That'.

ON-BOARD THE CG FRIGATE:
The PLA CG Commander has observed
everything that took place, through
binoculars, as he shouts his frustration. . .

"Son of a BITCH. . .He lied to us!"

ON-BOARD 'THE DRAGON' SUPERYACHT:
Tension is ratcheting up. It's a 'State of
Emergency'. The crew snaps to. . . as Jiang
yells out 'Orders'. . .

"Feed the Oxygen in . . . Longwei, man the
Monitors. . . This is no longer a 'Diving
Operation', but a 'Rescue Mission'. . ."

DEEPER UNDERWATER: The 'Rover'
Bathysphere makes its descent. Leaving
behind the surface. Lights slicing through
Darkness.

ON-BOARD 'THE DRAGON' SUPERYACHT:
Swells are splashing violently now as the
Storm reaches its peak velocity.
Jiang adds more directions from his years of
experience. . .
"We've got to hold 'The Dragon' steady.
Engage all 'Thrusters' and 'Stabilizers' both
Bow and Stern. . .
The CREWMEMBERS work the 'Manual' as
well as the 'Robotic" controls, video screens
and engine operations.
We see the 'Rover's View' on screen: mostly
dark.

Then the 'Readings Displays' inside the Rover.
. . Oxygen, Temperatures, Depth.
Once again, the inter-ship radio crackles. . .
As the CG COMMANDER, growls his
dissatisfaction. . .
"Jiang: you lied to us."

"Negative, Sir. Two rogue divers have
appropriated our 'ROVER' BATHYSPHERE.

The COMMANDER, disregards his answer. . .
"We're towing you to 'Shore'."

"Negative, Sir. If you do that, you 'SEVER'
their ONLY life-line. . .
I won't be accomplice to 'MURDER', even if
you do have wealthy friends."

The COMMANDER, hesitates, then answers. . .
"I don't know, Jiang. . .
This is truly a 'Stand-Off Situation'!'

"Acknowledged, Commander. However,
'SAFETY' is our Number-One concern now. . .
And Commander Liao. I know who's
controlling you, and it's got nothing to do with
your PLA Coast Guard Allegiance."

'Static' on the line. Blank. Decision time.
Jiang, finally breaks the 'Silence'. . .

"Give me an Hour, to get my 'Crew' back."

Static. . . Very Long Pause. . .Then --
The COMMANDER opens up with a calmer
tone. . .
"I can't compete with the Weather. The Swells
are too High. . . the Wind is too Harsh. . . we
can't Board under these Conditions. . .

It would endanger my Crew. . .
Aborting Operations. . .'OVER' and 'OUT'!"

At long last, Jiang smiles. 'Commander Liao's
one of 'The Good Guys' after all.'

Jiang's Master Crewman yells out the
'ROVER's' Status. . .
"They're below. . . Two-Hundred Meters.
Temp's dropped to Thirty-Seven Degrees.
They've visually found a 'Ledge'. . ."

Self-Propelled Oil Rig

Chapter 14

The Self-Propelled Oil Rig

The sky is turning an angry shade of black. Low clouds on the surface hiding a looming storm menace.

The first Helicopter slices along the Ocean surface. Exhaust heat distorting our overhead view. Razoring the top of the water in an up spray.

Then, a second Helicopter banks in, Positioning for a landing on. . . an Upper Deck Pad of a massive 'Self-Propelled Oil Rig'. The Monster crushes waves, as it 'Looms' right out of the Ocean moving at almost Ten-Knots toward the 'Dadong Dao Dive Exclusion Zone'.

The Monster is literally a massive city on stilts.

VanBoveen and his lead Operative jump out of the Second Helicopter with a contingent of SECURITY FORCES. . . including 'Hanna' and her 'Lead Backup'.
The SPO Rig's 'CAPTAIN' greets them. Then escorts them to the Control Deck for an Orientation. . .

"Gentlemen, what you see here is not unlike a Space Shuttle flying interstellar."

They quickly enter 'The bridge'. The nerve center. A bank of monitors and gadgets worth millions. VanBoveen observes, as the Navigation crews work the video screens and high tech controls, while the Rig's Captain ushers them through with more details. . .

"Contributing to forward movement, we have yaw, pitch, roll, vertical height, horizontal. . ."

Suddenly, VanBoveen interrupts. . .

"Captain, how quickly can you get over there and remove our assets?"

To that point, the Captain snaps and motions for the Operations Supervisor. . .

"We'll be over your 'Target' in less than thirty minutes. Our divers are on standby. . .
This Man beside me's from Houston Texas. . ."

He, at that, surrenders the floor. . .

To a hulking. . . 'Oil Rig Type'. . . Six-Foot-Five.
. . No Neck. . . Big Belly. . . the Man saunters
over and eyeballs VanBoveen. . .
He's what they call The 'TOOLPUSHER'. . .
begins commenting with a heavy Texas drawl.

"Fortunately, the information your people got
me early this morning, gave me enough
planning time to complete my modifications."

He grabs his 'Belly Fat' and moves it around
then continues. . .
"The divers will have a modified 'Mud Return
Pipe' at the target site to pull up your salvage --
VanBoveen raises his hand, bored with the
details. . .

"So, What, are we to expect?"

The 'Toolpusher' chuckles. . .
"Expect . . . Expect 'Some Ball-Crushing'
Machinery, Mercenary Type Penetration, and
a Snap Extraction. . . It's like we were NEVER
there."

As simplistic and crass, as this explanation is,
VanBoveen likes it. . .

"Okay, then! Get on with it!"

VanBoveen Turns to 'Hanna', as they leave the
Bridge. . .

ON-BOARD 'THE DRAGON' SUPERYACHT:
Viewing the sonar screen, an approaching massive blip is observed on the horizon. Papa Nui reacts, concerned. . .

"Unidentified, Boss."

Hang snaps up his binoculars. Scans, to the far distant vanishing point. . .

"You gotta be kidding me. . .!?"

DEEP BELOW UNDERWATER: The 'Rover' drifts downward into the surreal world of the Abyss, as Bohai watches the 'Radar Scope'. . .

"We should start seeing debris, soon. Take her in gently. . ."

Suddenly. . .

CRAAASH-BANG. . .
Their world instantly shudders, goes into a violent spinning motion. . .
Bohai and Meifeng grab the inside 'handle racks' of the 'Rover' and brace themselves against the unknown 'cause' of the power-full 'G-force'. . . Meifeng is terrified. . .

"What...was...that?"

Now everything has become serious, with the Bathysphere spinning out of control. . .
They're sinking into even darker depths. Melting into the Abyss. . .

"We're dropping fast, Meifeng. . . I can't locate us on the Radar either. . . Secure the --

WHAAM. . .
The tiny Bathysphere, grinds to a sickening halt.
They've hit something or something has hit them with a spine-jarring jolt. Damaged? Bruised?
Alarms are shrieking and flashing red, all around them. Deafening noise in such a small space.
Finally, Bohai hits all of the 'CANCEL' Buttons, Switches, Computer EXT's. . . and the 'Alarms' shut down. . . Replaced by an oppressive SILENCE. . .
Somehow, this feels worse to Bohai. . .

"What did we hit, Meifeng!?"

"Don't know?!"

"Something must have hit us, then, Mei?"

"I didn't do anything, Babe. There was nothing out there to hit.
We would have seen it on the. . .

The RADAR SCOPE BLIPS on and off. . . giving Bohai a glimpse to. . .

"We're on the 'Seafloor", I think. . .
But most probably, a 'Shelf'. I know the Abyss goes much deeper. . .

"I know that, too."

"Meifeng, if we're at the edge of the Abyss,
then the current could drag us off, even below
our CRUSH Depth. We'll never see daylight
again.

Bohai tries the ignition sequence.
The ROVER struggles. The engine WHIRRS.
Light suddenly floods, inside the cramped
cabin space. They breathe relief. . .

"Bohai. . . the words DIE on her lips. . ."

"What, Babe. . .!?"

He follows her stare out. . .
The 'Main Porthole'. . .
To a massive drifting, solid, impenetrable
object kicking up silt. . .

It's an enormous 'Orange Tube', with an Oil
Company Decal. No end in sight.
Bohai and Meifeng stare dumbfounded.
They can't even react, they're so stunned.

When Bohai, at last, lets out his butt joke . . .

"Son of a 'Pig Bitch'!"

"What?"

"Your 'Criminal Bankers' are HERE."

Then he realizes. . . it's still 'MOVING'!

"No . . . No WAY. . . Oh 'FUCK'. . ."

What? What's 'HAPPENING', Bohai?"

"Brace! It's coming straight at us. . ."

A 'GIANT' Orange Pipe Opening, fills the
porthole view. . . Everything, sand, silt, debris,
and now the even the 'Beebe is 'sucking into it!

BANG. . .
Again, the world is spinning around in nausea
inducing flips. . .

The 'GIANT' Orange Pipeline extends back
upward all the way to the surface. . .
But now, it has somehow snagged the little
'Beebe-Rover', dragging and scraping it, along
the SHELF bottom. . .
While Bohai and Meifeng are again, thrown
around violently inside.

Chapter 15

The Final Confrontation

OCEAN SURFACE AT DADONG DAO ISLET:
As we follow the mammoth length 'Orange
Tube' upward, we arrive at the Self-Propelled
Mobile 'OIL RIG' Platform. . .

Oil Rigging Equipment, Pipes, Ballast Hulls
and Metal Frames dwarf, 'The Dragon'
Superyacht by almost a Hundred-Meters. . .as
Jiang roars out!

"They're going to ram us!"

But, the platform abruptly, stops DEAD in the
water, only meters away from a collision.

Unaware of the chaos it has caused under the
sea's surface. . .

DEEP BELOW UNDERWATER - THE ROVER:
Cascading crazy. Bohai and Meifeng struggle
to regain any control. But now they are even
fighting against pressure crushing in on them.

BRIDGE - 'THE DRAGON' SUPERYACHT:
Longwei, Jiang and Guozhi watch with mouths
open, as Colonel Longwei is the first to walk
out On-Deck to confront the 'Monsters'. . .

"You gotta be kidding me."

ON THE OIL RIG – AT A DECK OVERLOOK:
VanBoveen is looking down at 'The Dragon' as
he begins speaking in a Hand Microphone. . .

"Yacht, 'DRAGON' . . .
BE AWARE. . .
You are 'Trespassing', Gentlemen!"

BRIDGE - 'THE DRAGON' SUPERYACHT:
Papa Nui is the first to hear something faint,
buried in a 'Burst of Static' from the radio.

"Sounds like Bohai and Meifeng. Screaming.
But it 'winks out'. Too short to tell. . . "

Papa Nui approaches Hang, but Hang's still
awestruck by the oil rig perched over them. . .

"Do you realize how much those damn things
are worth?"

ON THE OIL RIG – AT A DECK OVERLOOK:
VanBoveen shouts in his 'Mic' at 'The Dragon'!

"We have 'Legal PRC Documents' for your
perusal. You are invited to 'Board' our 'RIG'
and assess them yourself. . .

INSIDE THE BRIDGE - 'THE DRAGON':
Guozhi shouts Orders to the Crew. . .
"Tell them to Fuck-off. . . I'm Guozhi Hang.
XO of this Superyacht. And I'm not
stepping on that monster."

ON THE OIL RIG – AT A DECK OVERLOOK:
VanBoveen again shouts in his 'Mic'. . .

"Listen to me, Gentlemen, this is a 'Final Warning'. . . You're NOW 'Trespassing' in this Ten-Kilometer Zone. . ."

ON-DECK OUTSIDE - 'THE DRAGON'S' BRIDGE: Guozhi Hang walks out of the Bridge Control Room himself and uses his Megaphone. . .

"All right, up there, All RIGHT. But give us at least Two-Hours. . .
We've got Divers down in the Abyss and we need time to pull them up. . .

ON THE OIL RIG - DECK OVERLOOK:
VanBoveen seems to give in as he again shouts in his 'Mic'. . .

"OKAY. . . You've got NINETY Minutes. 'No More'. . .
And XO Hang. . . Any deception on your part; 'KNOW', that we have the 'Authority to Fire' on your Boat. . . 'Without Warning'. . ."

VanBoveen waves his HAND, and his own Deck Crew uncovers a 'FIFTY-Caliber Machinegun'. . . It's pointed directly at. . .
'The Dragon's' Bridge'. . . 'Gotchya'!

DEEP BELOW UNDERWATER - THE ROVER:
Silt is beginning to settle outside the porthole.

The 'Rover' now rests upside down. . .
It's Leaking. Just a hairline, but DEADLY.

Bohai's bullet wound is bleeding again.
He's disoriented. They're BOTH shell shocked,
'Ghostlike Faces'.

Bohai softly speaks to Meifeng. . .

"Seems like it's stopped for now. Get Hang on
the radio. . ."

The 'Rover' groans under the pressure impact.

INSIDE THE BRIDGE - 'THE DRAGON':
Papa Nui on the radio to the 'Beebe'. . .

"Over. . . I can't get through, Boss."

He checks the Radar Scope. The Sonar.
Something's wrong. Coordinates?

"Something's happened. They've changed
position."

Guozhi Hang jumps in clearly alarmed. . .

"Whatya mean, 'Papa'. . . they've changed
Position!?
. . . They can't just change position."

Hang eyes his Sonar. . . then the Charts.
Papa Nui does the same with his Scopes. . .

"They're off by. . ."

. . . A 'FULL' Kilometer, 'Papa'. How the crap
did they get that far off-course?"

"Boss, that puts them 'right smack' on the edge
of. . ."
Papa Nui circles the main chart sheet with a
wax pen. . . at a place where the undersea
'Clift' drops into nothingness. . .

"It's black ink. . . from that point. . .
into the. . ."

Shocked, Hang stares. . .at Papa Nui. . .then
the darkening sky outside. . .
That 'DAMN' Abyss. . .

ON-DECK OUTSIDE - 'THE DRAGON'S'
BRIDGE: Guozhi Hang walks out of the
'Bridge Control Room' watching as Two Zodiac
type inflatables launch from the Oil Rig. . .

"Damn, They're going after that CG Frigate to
get us ejected from the Zone!
On cue, Papa Nui rushes out of the Bridge.

"I still can't get through. Their Radio must be
out. And our 'on-board' computer's glitching,
with some kind of interference, too."

"What else, do we know, Papa?"

Longwei walks up. Grim faced. He's heard
everything. . .he speaks ominously. . .

"They're running out of time. Get a 'Ready
Boat' to their vertical position on the surface."

DEEP BELOW UNDERWATER - THE ROVER:
Something else is outside as. . .

THWACK...
Meifeng crawls past Bohai. . . in a trance, as if
she's seen a ghost. . .
She's gripped by something outside. . .
Looking out the PORTHOLE. . .
He joins her, as they both stare out, with the
silt blur, finally disintegrating . . . revealing. . .

A SILHOUETTE . . . A MATSU CLASS
DESTROYER - The KABA. . .
A massive gash in her hull with part of her
cargo of 'Gold Storage Crates' spread-out in a
wide debris field. . .

Instantly. . . Bohai and Meifeng are
Mesmerized. . .
Silly grins appear on their faces.
Only the 'Archeologist' who discovered the
'Terracotta Army of Emperor Huang'
understands their awe. . .

"There she is, Mei."

Suddenly a sickening CRACK. . .

Oh Gawd. . .What was that, Babe. . .
What in 'Hell' is NEXT for us?"

"Stay calm, Mei. Breathe slowly."

Two hairline fissures are rapidly spouting
water. Bohai jolts into gear. . .

"We've gotta find the 'Escape Diving Suits'."

"Diving Suits? But wait, Bohai!"

"We're evacuating, Mei. . .NOW!"

Meifeng chokes on his announcement. . .

"Swim up? We're more than Eight-Hundred-Meters Down, Bohai. . .
No one can survive a 'Free Assent' from this depth. We'll get Crushed, plus 'Narcs' too."

"Mei, if we stay, we DIE."

"Even if we survive. . . I don't want to imagine spending the rest of my life eating through a tube."

At that moment, another fissure ERUPTS. . .
With total, full-bodied panic gripping Meifeng. Like a smack across the face, it freezes her.

"We're already DEAD. Another crack in that window and . . . we're. . ."

'He Can't say it.' Emotions tumbling in his mind. Bohai clutches her against him. Holds her there. The capsule around them CREAKING. . .
Their bodies are shaking. He can't let go. Their eyes meet. Both of them pale, cold, shivering.

And somehow, within each other's eyes, they find the strength to do the impossible. . .

"Hey, Babe. . . You're 'The Boy who Rode the Dragon'. You're the one that can do it!"

"Hah. Rode 'Down to the Gold', but couldn't touch it."

"Yet we found the KABA, Babe. With massive tons of your 'Dragon Treasure'."

His eyes well up, as his 'sarcasm', turns back to 'Sincerity'. No Regrets. . .

"Find the Suits, Mei. We've gotta go."

She nods. . . 'Accepting the End'. Accepting this might, 'Not Work'. . .
She hides it all, with her electrifying smile.

"Okay, then. . . Let's do it, Babe!"

INSIDE THE BRIDGE - 'THE DRAGON':
Papa Nui still on the radio to reach the 'Beebe'.
Guozhi Hang grabs the radio mic. . .changes
the dial-in to the SP Oil Rig and shouts his
request. . .

We sincerely need your help Mr. VanBoveen,
It's an EMERGENCY. . .

IN THE OIL RIG – CONTROL ROOM:
VanBoveen reluctantly answers. . .
"Yes."

INSIDE THE BRIDGE - 'THE DRAGON':
Guozhi Hang points out his situation. . .

"Two of our Divers might be stranded."

IN THE OIL RIG – CONTROL ROOM:
VanBoveen seethes his response . . .

"A ploy XO Hang, to buy time while your
Divers scavenge the seafloor?"

INSIDE THE BRIDGE - 'THE DRAGON':
Guozhi Hang gets sarcastic. . .

"Now what would they be scavenging for?"

IN THE OIL RIG – CONTROL ROOM:
VanBoveen jokes back . . .

"Clearly, 'A myth'?"

INSIDE THE BRIDGE - 'THE DRAGON':
Guozhi Hang adds a thought . . .

"Is this why you've brought an entire 'Self-Propelled Oil Platform' HERE . . . 'For a Myth'?
Hang is back to serious. . .
"Fact is we haven't heard back from our divers in two hours. . .
Their instruments are off-line, as well.
We need to. . . I mean 'could we borrow' one of your 'Submersibles'?"

Long silence. A twinge of hope appears in Hang's eyes. . .

'Static' . . . Then the flat reply. . .

IN THE OIL RIG – CONTROL ROOM:
VanBoveen finally reacts . . .
"No."
'Static Increases. . . Then the 'Radio' turns off.

INSIDE THE BRIDGE - 'THE DRAGON':
Guozhi Hang chokes his words . . .

"Sunofabitch!"

Hang runs out on Deck to get air. . .

IN THE OIL RIG – CONTROL ROOM:
VanBoveen looks over his shoulder at. . .
'Hanna' as he shouts . . .

"Shut them down! NOW!"

FORWARD BRIDGE DECK - 'THE DRAGON':
Guozhi watches the Oil Rig's 'Lower Sea Deck'
as VanBoveen's men begin sealing the hatches
on both their submersibles to Dive.
Guozhi starts ranting out loud. . .
"They can't do this. They're going against
International Maritime law. . .
They MUST answer all distress calls."

OUTSIDE THE OIL RIG – ON-DECK:
VanBoveen takes a final vicious look at XO
Hang ranting away on 'The Dragon', as he
'Fists' his Operative Teams, from the Oil Rig's
Overlook. . .

Chapter 16

A Death in the Abyss

DEEP BELOW UNDERWATER - THE ROVER:
Water rising. Temperatures dropping fast.

"We have to flood the 'ROVER'. NOW, Mei!"

"No."

**"We MUST balance the pressure. . . then we
fire the last 'Buoyancy Thruster'.
That should shave off One-Hundred Meters.
When that 'Thruster' fails, we open the hatch."**

**Meifeng falls quiet. Thinking seriously
technical about that plan. . .**

**"We're too close, Babe. If you fire the
'Thruster', the extra pressure will push that
Destroyer off the fragile ledge."**

Bohai thinks about that realty . . .

**"You'll lose the KABA, Forever Babe. The last
hope of your family's legacy."**

Meanwhile, unknown to Meifeng or Bohai. . .

UNDER THE OIL RIG – IN DEEP-WATER:
**Two submersibles from the Rig rapidly
penetrate deeper. . .
Down to the shelf where the KABA is located.**

INSIDE THE BRIDGE - 'THE DRAGON':
Colonel Longwei turns away from watching
XO Hang's useless effort through a Bridge
Port Hole, in frustration when. . .

BANG. . .
A round, slices through his shoulder.
Dumb struck, his fingers find the smoking
hole.
Looks up to find. . .
The ultimate assassin, 'HANNA'. . .
Berretta in hand.
It's leveled at Longwei's head. And just when
you'd expect a shot to go off again. . .

THWACK. . .
Daiyu sidekicks Hanna in the ribs, sending her
flying against the wall. . .
The two combatants size each other up. . .
Circle each other in the 'Close Space' of the
Bridge as Hanna dive bombs three hooks.

Daiyu swings, dips and connects two jabs into
her ribs. Sending Hanna tumbling back. The
antes are up. . .
Both baying for blood. Hanna attacks with
primal fury. . .

CRUSHED. . .
Daiyu flies into the far wall. . .

DEEP BELOW UNDERWATER - THE ROVER:
Now, water has entered to their waist level as
the failing 'Rover' GROANS. . .
Just then, the main 'Porthole' spider-webs. . .
Meifeng at last pulls out a diving suit complete
with helmet and two oxygen tanks. . .
She struggles locating the second suit then. . .

Her head drifts up, as if she's seen death itself.

"What is it, Mei?"

She leans back in a sitting position. All hope
abandoned.

"Come on. . .What is it?"

He starts to rummage through the two diving
suit cases.

"It's no use. . .there's only one diving helmet
and no back-up tanks. . ."

More GROANING. The BEEBE'S capsule shifts
another foot. The lights flicker.
It's like that 'Moment on the Titanic', as the
Ship begins to slide down into the deep. . .
Meifeng has tears in her eyes, lips quivering -

"One of us, can't make it."

Unyielding. The obvious choice all along;
Bohai smiles at her. . .

"You Go. My shoulder's still shot!"

"You're the stronger swimmer, Babe. You
might survive. Go. . ."

She's on her feet. Confronting him. Lips vibrating and blue from the icy water. Suddenly angry; Bohai demands her. . .

"You Go!"

Meifeng is resolute. . .

"No!"

"Why d' you have to be so stubborn all the time, Mei?   You never listen to me. Ever!"

"It's the logical thing, Babe."

Water continues rising – It's Biting cold. Frigid. . .

"Crap on Logic!"

"Even now you're too 'Pigheaded' to admit, I'm Right."

Water level climbing. . . chaos all around them. But instead of fighting back, Meifeng grows gentle, serene, calm. . .

"Bohai...listen to me... listen: I was wrong not to marry you. I see that now. I'm not right all the time. But I'm right, now."

Bohai laughs in pure frustration. She guides his eyes into hers.

"It's the ONLY thing left to do, Babe."

INSIDE THE BRIDGE - 'THE DRAGON':
Colonel Longwei is out of the fray, still tending
to his chest wound. . .watching as. . .
Daiyu scrapes herself up.
Daiyu attacks. Shields and Shin Kicks. Shields
and Punches. Never breaking stride. No
wasted moves, no wasted breath. They
pummel each other in a dizzying blur of speed.

The women plow into each other, madly.
Lashing out in daemonic fury. . .

Suddenly, Hanna gets the upper hand. Pelting
Daiyu, unrelenting.
Driving her down. Pummeling her into the
floor. Daiyu balls herself into a savage knot of
kicks and strikes.
Then in a hideous battle cry, she Football
tackles Hanna pushing her through the side
window. . .

As this happens: Daiyu realizes Hanna will fall
to her death on the deck below. . . a sheer
Eight-Meter drop. . .
For some unknown, she latches to Hanna's
wrists. They dangle there. Arms straining. The
pressure immense. What to do next.
They lock eyes. . .
Like Two Ancient Amazon Warriors, knowing
the end is nigh . . .

Then, Daiyu calls out to her. . .
"Use your feet. I'll swing you to the right. Drop
on that ledge. . .
Hanna leers.
This is against her code. She reaches back and
pulls out a '9mm GLOCK'.

BLAAM-BLAAM.
Firing blind. Bullets whistle past Daiyu's head
As Hanna lets go, still firing.
Her eyes never leave Daiyu's.
Dropping away. Fast. Bullets blasting. Loyal to
the code. . .then. . .

SPLAT
Daiyu looks away. A twisted mess of blood. It's
over. . . the destruction of a 'Beautiful Foe'.

DEEP BELOW UNDERWATER - THE ROVER:
They're at last, suited in the freezing seawater
that's now up to their chests. Bohai's helmet is
on. Meifeng suddenly has horror on her face.

"Bohai . . . we're upside down."

On the floor. . .water is spewing upward. No
air pockets.

"The hatch is under us."

"We're okay. . . There's an emergency hatch.
We'll have to blow it open.   '

Bohai falls silent. He takes his helmet off.

"What are you doing, Babe?

"I can't do this. You stay, I stay."

"Bohai. . .

"Though I want to set you on FIRE, sometimes
You're. . . my home."

And just then, something bobs to the surface.
. . . Another diving helmet.

"You gotta be kidding?"

"Here goes. . .Babe"

Cold spiking through her, Meifeng dives
under. Rummages. She resurfaces. . .
With the extra oxygen tanks.

"I've got them. . .We can do this."

"Put your helmet on, Babe!"

She empties the helmet. Tries to lock it in
place. . .

"My fingers are too stiff."

Bohai helps her. Rigs the tanks. Seals the
helmet. Presses the flush. Just in time. Water
is now halfway up their helmets.
As . . . they submerge. . .

Once under, they thumb each other.
Bohai then breaks the glass of a safety panel,
And 'Presses the Red' button, as the entire
capsule comes alive. . .

The ballast thruster bursts open sending a
blast of bubbles and silt outward. Causing the
'Rover' to spins on itself, like a 'headless
chicken'.

For the Two of them, the world swirls away in
messy circles. Finally, Bohai wrestles the
direction levers as they redirect 'The Beebe'
upward an hopefully home. . .

The bathysphere rooster-tales upward in a
continuous blast. But that shift of seawater is
too powerful, rocking the Destroyer's unstable
hull off its shelf anchorage.

Through the splintered Porthole at their feet,
they watch as. . . the KABA breaks away from
the cliff and begins its slow slide into the
Abyss.
Lost forever and in ghostly silence, the
darkness of the Abyss, swallows it up. . .

Chapter 17

The Recovery

INSIDE THE BRIDGE - 'THE DRAGON':
Daiyu immediately tends to Colonel Longwei's chest wound. A clean shot. Right through the back. Mostly muscle.
The bridge is a mess. Jiang massages his own bruised ribs.
Then, he notices the radar sweeping. It's picking up something. A blip!
Papa Nui runs in. No time to ask questions or comment on the chaotic mess on the Bridge. . .

"We got something, Boss."

"What is it?"

"It's coming up. Half a mile out."
Papa Nui stares out to sea. As if, he could actually see Bohai and Meifeng on the horizon.

"Crew!   Sonofabitch . . . Get a boat out there."

DEEP BELOW UNDERWATER - THE ROVER:
It begins as a pinpoint light. Grows in size.
Heading this way. A minuscule speck against a deep and dark trench. . .then. . .

SSCCHWWUUIISSHHH
It rockets up toward the surface, whipping a swirling contrail of bubbles.
Not there yet, it's still in 'Deep Black Ocean', but it's on the way. . .

OUTSIDE THE LAUNCH DECK:
Guozhi Hang and Papa Nui jump into a high
speed 'Launch' docked on the Superyacht's
Stern. . .
OVERHEAD - ON THE OIL RIG DECK:
Vanboveen is yelling into his megaphone as
his .50 Caliber Machine Gunner charges the
GUN.
"You are restricted to your Yacht."
You are 'Trespassing'. We WILL fire!"

OUTSIDE THE STERN LAUNCH DECK:
Guozhi Hang reacts, but only Papa Nui can
hear him. . .

"Trespassing? The Bastard."

Papa Nui stares in fear at Guozhi, then the Rig.

"Boss. . . Commander . . . Wait?"

In defiance, Guozhi Hang tests VanBoveen.
He ignites the Launch's turbo-jet engines as. . .

RATRATRATRATRAT
A rooster tail of water 'fountains' up on deck,
missing them by inches. . .
This time, Guozhi shouts up at Vanboveen.

"Okay. . . Okay!   Cease Firing."

As they stop firing, he continues. . .

"We've got Two Divers coming up. . .
Condition Unknown, 'Assumed Critical'.
It's an EMERGENCY and they need our help."

OVERHEAD - ON THE OIL RIG DECK:
Vanboveen reacts. . .

"Are they bringing up CARGO?"

OUTSIDE THE 'DRAGON'S' LAUNCH DECK:
Guozhi gives a nervous laugh. . .
"What are you taking about?"

OVERHEAD - ON THE OIL RIG DECK:
"Have they found anything, Hang?"

OUTSIDE THE 'DRAGON'S' LAUNCH DECK:
"NO . . . Why is that important? They've lost
their BATHYSHPERE. . .
They're in 'Free Assent'. . ."

OVERHEAD - ON THE OIL RIG DECK:
VanBoveen and his men exchange looks.
"What?"
Did they hear right?
'That's lunacy.'
'They're NOT carrying cargo. . .'

Finally, Vanboveen 'Yells' back. . .

"Then they are of 'NO CONCERN' to us."

Vanboveen turns to his Gunner and motions
for him to 'Stand Down'. . .

"Carry On Then, Hang!"

OUTSIDE THE 'DRAGON'S' LAUNCH DECK:
Guozhi Hang and Papa Nui stare at the
gasoline stain drifting away from the 'Launch'.
The bullet holes in side wall of the Boat, tell it
all. . . it's a lost cause, the tanks are ruptured.
Then, Papa Nui sees a 'Fancy Wave Runner'
parked in the 'Toys Storage'. . . he slides it out
and straps it to the Yacht's stern deck.

Hang reacts. . .
"That's not big enough. . ."

As Papa Nui corrects him. . .
"It's all we've got. . . I'll need room for medical
supplies. And two people. . .this'll have to do!

CLOSER NOW- UNDERWATER - THE ROVER:
Bohai and Meifeng. Faces distorted against the
incredible pressure elements. The world
around them a violent tremor.
The Rover's thrusters skip and cough.
It's running out of power.

Finally, the thrusters cough out their last
breath. The rover stalls. Then begins to drift
downward. . .

Bohai pulls on the Release Lever. Hard. But it
won't budge. Meifeng helps him, then cracks
the safety panel, as it explodes out.

They barely have time to hold onto each other
when they get sucked out in a great torrent.
They bump the side and. . .

SWOOOSH...

The 'Rover' sheers away from them. They're spat out. Into the great blackness of the ocean.

As the rover peels away and disappears down in the darkness, Meifeng notices beads of air leaking out of Bohai's oxygen hose. The gauge needle teasing red. He won't make it.

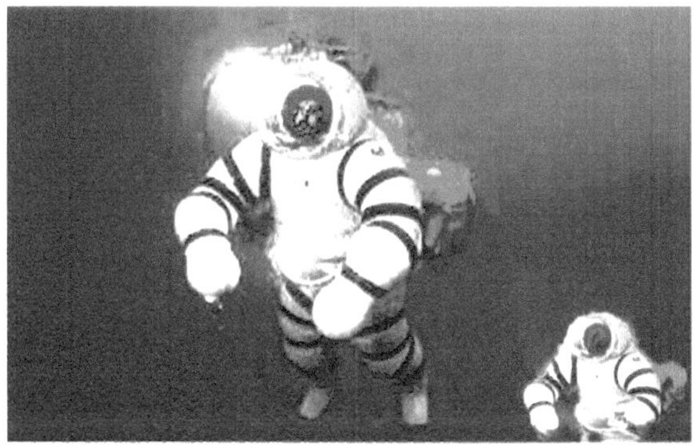

Deep Water - Pressurized Escape Suits

CONTROL BRIDGE - THE SP OIL RIG:
A Technician points out the sonar image to VanBoveen. . .

"We've located the Destroyer's wreck, Sir."

"And their ROVER?"

Two blips show up on screen. . .

VanBoveen issues orders. . .

"Commence Recovery of the KABA."

"And the ROVER, Sir?"

"We never saw it."

The technician suddenly jerks to attention. Staring at his sonar screen. Not believing what he's seeing. . .

"Heir VanBoveen."

"Yes?"

"The KABA has...disappeared?!"

"What?"
Stares at the sonar screen.

"How is that even possible?"

The technician opens his mouth to answer, but he's frozen with fear. . .

"It can't disappear. Find it, NOW!"

VanBoveen looks out to sea in the opposite direction as. . .

OPEN SEA – NEAR DADONG DAO:
Papa Nui rips the waves on the 'Wave Runner'. He's too far out to be caught by the Gunner. Laughing like the demented Mariner riding 'Moby Dick' to his death. . .

UNDERWATER – GAINING TO SURFACE:
The water has turned a paler shade of blue.
But Bohai and Meifeng are still too far down to
see any sign of surface light.

They spear upwards. Bohai's hose pipes now
gushing oxygen. The needle on the gauge
firmly stuck halfway in red. . .

OPEN SEA – NEAR DADONG DAO:
Papa Nui reads his GPS. He circles the spot
where he thinks they'll be surfacing.
Reading the water for signs of life. . .

"Come' on . . . Come' on Kiddos, Come' on. . ."

Suddenly, Static . . . then Screeching in his
headset. . . it's XO Hang. . .

"You've got 'Visitors'."

Papa Nui looks up. 'Trouble!' Boats rushing
from the Oil Rig his way. . .

RISING BUT STILL UNDERWATER: Meifeng
and Bohai drift upward. They catch sight of
each other. Love separated by face shields.
Bohai has 'No Oxygen' left. . .

OPEN SEA – NEAR DADONG DAO:
The Two SP Oil Rig Boats approach. . .
Papa Nui jumps several waves as he gets ahead
of them. . .
"Here we go. . ."

He pegs the accelerator. The jet ski turbos out in the opposite direction. The chase is on. Both SP RIG Boats bite. . .

RISING - BUT STILL UNDERWATER:
Bohai drifts in and out of consciousness. Meifeng slaps his mask to wake him up. Shouting in her mask. For a moment, we're in her mask. Her voice confined in this plastic coffin.

"Bohai. . . Bohai. Stay with me. Don't do this, Bohai. Bohai. Bohai!"

Panic in her voice. It's heart-wrenching.

OUTSIDE DECK - THE SP OIL RIG:
On deck, VanBoveen watches his boats give chase.
UNDER THE RIG PLATFORM:
Undetected. . . Guozhi Hang sneaks onto VanBoveen's unguarded Italian Cigarette Race Boat, moored to the Oil Rig. He keys the ignition. Drops it in gear. And fires up the big jets engines. . .

EXPLODING out of there with a blasting **ROAR. . .**

RISING UNDERWATER – NEAR SURFACE:
She starts seeing the surface now. Bohai is limp. Meifeng in panic. Clawing at the water to climb faster.

BRIDGE DECK - THE SP OIL RIG:
VanBoveen cuts a cruel scowl seeing his Super
'Play Toy' screaming out to sea.
He's really starting to hate these people.

OPEN SEA – NEAR DADONG DAO:
Guozhi Hang giggles to himself, revving the
engine, a lit Cuban piping out of his clenched
teeth and firing bright in the rushing wind.

UNDERWATER – NEARING SUNLIGHT:
Meifeng dragging Bohai and aiming for the
star of sunlight breaking the surface. And then
she sees it. . . a speedboat.
Hope renewed. Her arms piston upward.
Yelling in her mask.
The speedboat circles and . . .
Drives off. Leaving behind a 'White Wake' of
water.
Meifeng freaks. . .

"NO . . . NO OHHH!"

She doubles her effort. Pedaling. Arms heavy
with fatigue. But her sheer determination and
spirit is overwhelming. . .

OPEN SEA – NEAR DADONG DAO:
Guozhi Hang checks the Speedboat's GPS.
Then the horizon. . .
"Can't see a thing. Damn."

BREACHING TO SUNLIGHT:
Blood gushes out of Meifeng's nose. Clawing
and she suddenly. . .

. . . Breaches the surface in an incredible
splash of water.
Limbs thrashing on fire. Her body gives out.

She unlocks Bohai's helmet. Leans him back to
float. But he's gone. Unresponsive. Lips
purple.
She rips off her helmet and sucks in a huge
gulp of air. The primal breath. Burning her
lungs.

"Bohai. . . Bohai . . .We made it. . .
We made it.
Stay with me."

Then she looks out to sea. Nothing across her
horizon. She's too low on the surface. Waves
blocking. . .
"No. No. Where are they!"

Waves break. The sea stretches forever. No
rescue in sight.

"NO . . . NO . . . OOHHH!"

She's too far out. No one can save her. They're
doomed.
With her one cry of despair and agony. . .
She weeps. . .
Suddenly. She hears something. Something
far off. Coming this way. The rumble of water.
The waves break over her then. . .
She turns around to find. . .
Guozhi Hang. He's less than a Fifty Meters
away. Racing at her. . .

DECK OF VANBOVEEN'S CIGARETTE: MOMENTS LATER. . . Bohai's splayed on the boat's deck. Hang cuts through his dive suit.

"Come on, Bohai. Breathe Man!"

Meifeng lays absolutely wasted on deck.
Too spent to sit up.
Hang begins CPR. Pumps Bohai's chest. Breathing compressions. Working like a madman. But he's not responding. No signs of life. No twitching. No gasping. It's been too long now.

"Meifeng. I know you're exhausted. But you need to work with me here. I need your help. Get me that cylinder of oxygen, NOW."

Don't ask how, but somehow Meifeng crawls across the deck to fetch the oxygen cylinder and passes it to Hang.
He straps the oxygen mask on Bohai. Cranks the flowmeter.
Oxygen pumps straight into Bohai's lungs. His chest rises. But nothing.
Fearing the worse, time completely grinds to a halt. The world around them ceases to exist. The sun is too shiny. Sounds distort. Hang pumps away. His arms tiring fast.

"Come on, Bohai. Wake up, BOY!"
Hang pushes back.
Exhausted. Doesn't want to give up.
Meifeng screams out. . .
"NO. NO. DON'T STOP!"

"It's Been too long. It's over Meifeng."

And in that terrible silence. . .

Meifeng lets out a 'Primal SCREAM of Agony'
then crawls violently to Bohai.
She's 'Beating on his Chest'. . .yelling at him.

"Bohai, you son of a bitch. You've never given
up in your entire life.
Don't give up now.
Come back, come back!"

And then she says IT . . . the only words that
echo deeply enough to enter through his ears
into his MIND in his coma induced state. . .
Meifeng whimpers to him sadly. . .

"Come back, Bohai. . .
Come back to MEEEE. . ."

Maybe it's the beating on his chest, maybe it's
the words, but Bohai suddenly erupts water
from his lungs.
Twists in agony. Coughing and sputtering.
Struggling to breathe. Meifeng and Hang stare
in shock. . .
They've just witnessed a 'Miracle'.

WIDE VIEW OF THE SCENE:
We leave them alone now. . . as
Meifeng assists Bohai to recovery. . .

Chapter 18

Haughton's Surprise

Haughton's Hong Kong Estate

HONG KONG ESTATE - LATE AFTERNOON:
A Mozart Quartet is softly playing selections to create the perfect musical atmosphere throughout the Estate's Living and Dining areas.
Haughton himself is entertaining his guests: Industrialists. World Bankers. Industry Captains: Americans, British, Germans, Japanese, Swiss. Lots of money here.
Old money.
A lavish Henry VIII type buffet has been laid out. . .
Haughton is sitting at the head of the table, giving his guests the lowdown. . .

"I can assure ALL, your investment is well

protected. The American Banks and those of Switzerland assure me of a colossal return for this 'Gold Bullion'. Nevertheless, my man on the ground informed me that 'The Kaba'. . ."

A PERSONAL ASSISTANT interrupts him. Whispers into his ear. . .

A dreadful pause descends into a thick silence. Haughton's face changes color from pink to purple.
He erupts one single, universal word of defeat

"HELL!
TO HELL with all of them!!"

Startling his distinguished guests into absolute fear . . .

Chapter 19

The Professor's Revelation

THE CEMETERY- SHANGHAI, CHINA:
Time forward - One Week Later. Evening.
Two silhouettes. Standing at a Grave under a
weeping willow tree.

GRAVE MARKER: 'Professor Yafeng Zhang'.

Bohai's leaning on a crutch; we can tell his near-death experience has spooked him for once. His right shoulder is bandaged. His gaze fixes, the Sea 'shimmering like diamonds' on the evening horizon.

His 'Treasure and Family's Revenge', Lost to the Abyss, somewhere out there forever.

Meifeng squeezes his hand. He surrenders a gentle smile. . .

After a long silence, reading his mind. . .

"You know, that 'Gold' wasn't ours, Babe."

Bohai thinks on that. Finally nods . . .
Deep down, he knows. she's right.

"The 'Gold and those Jewels' belong to the Chinese people. To everybody and anybody who had the misfortune of crossing Hirohito's path on all the lands of Asia."

He's listening, as she interjects . . .

"But, there's just one thing I don't get?"

"What's that, Mei?"

"That time we visited that 'Old German, Mr. Braun', his nurse was quite adamant. . .
When she, at first, thought and said, 'his boat sank near Lingshan Island'. . ."

And . . . What are you getting at?"

"That 'Island' is actually, due South of Dadong Dao. And it's never been surveyed for those underground 'Japanese Forge Factories' either?"

"So, what are you thinking?"

"Maybe in the past because they were 'Off-the-Mainland' islands, they were BOTH used for 'Forging Gold Bullion'. . .
Maybe Mr. Braun knew that."

Slowly a curious, puzzled look descends on Bohai. . .
A hundred gears begin churning in his head, to create an idea. . .

"What if?   What. . . IF?"

He bolts, as much as a man can bolt on crutches. . . Meifeng is shocked at his sudden agility. . .

"Hey. Wait. . .Babe . . ."

. . . She smiles at him!

". . . for Me!"

THE MARITIME MUSEUM: Later that Night. Bohai 'speed-marches' on the lawn toward the Entrance. It's still Open for Students. . .

Meifeng is hot on his heels.

THE WAR LIBRARY - MARITIME MUSEUM: Shelves canyon around them, as Bohai whizzes by rows of books.

"Professor Zhang once said that 'Ninety-Nine' percent of 'Archeology' was done. . ."

Meifeng answers for him. . .

". . .in the Library!"

SPECIAL ARCHIVES SECTION :
Rows upon rows of gray boxes. This is where they store the 'Ancient Manuscripts'.

"He also said that 'The further back you go, the more history resembles some kind of Faerie Tale', rather than solid TRUTH. . ."

And there. He finds the row.

"Look for. . . HT **09-12-72** . . ."

"The Markings on the 'Second Diary', Babe?"

"No . . . the markings in 'Blood on his floor. . . Hey, YOU looked at the diary, too?"

"Snuck a peak, before you."

Bohai can't help but smile. . .

"Start at that end. . ."

They separate. Starting at each end. Fingers sweeping over book spines and boxes.

"What exactly am I looking for?"

A strange, calm disbelief lights up Bohai's face. . .

"The coordinates of his 'Last Dig'."

Their Eyes, rapidly scanning numbers.

"Professor Zhang would have known the truth of those 'Island Slave Labor Forges'. . ."

Working their way down row after row. . .

"Hiroshima and Nagasaki brought the WAR crashing down on Japan. They had to quickly evacuate the unprocessed 'Gold and Jewels' from China and turn it into untraceable 'Gold Bullion Bars'. The Forges had to be protected, near but not on, the Mainland. . ."

Meifeng has a mental 'Epiphany' herself. . .

"What if that 'Destroyer' was 'Empty' and its 'Treasure' was already at a 'Forge Plant' being processed?"

Hands running over boxes. Numbers racing past them. . .as she adds to her conclusion.

"Three islands are nearby the Port of Qingdao:
Dadong Dao, The Islands near Dashi Island
and finally Lingshan. . .

"But only Dadong Dao had a KNOWN Forge."

Bohai adds the 'What if. . .'
Excitement is mounting.

"What IF . . . Professor Zhang found another
Forge located on Lingshan Island!"

Both their hands land on the same 'Box', at the
same MOMENT!
A supercharged, intimate beat, holds between
them. . .

THE BOX: They spread the contents open on a
work table. . .
Frantic hands, carefully sift through the 'Old
Artifacts';   Japanese Infantry items. A Comb.
A Patch. A Photo of a Sweetheart. A Homeland
Photo. Poignant. The emotional weight not
lost on them. . .

"Something has to be HERE!"

'Ah-ha.' She finds it. Unfolds a creased, stiff
sheet. A Japanese Map of the East Coast of
China. The Yellow Sea.
Meifeng eyeballs the Map closely. . .

"What's this   'X'   ?"

"Mei! That's it!   The 'Actual' Coordinates:

'35.45'.33.9 North' by
                        '120. 10'.4 East'

This has to be the Underground Forge Entrance. . .”

Bohai is finally relieved, but intense. . .

“It was ‘Blown-Up’ with all the Slave Laborers and Bullion, left inside for a future return.

Maybe even including, some of ‘My Relatives’, that lost their ‘Gold and Treasure’ to ‘Japan's Empire of Terror’!”

Chapter 20

The Ultimate Discovery

AN EASTERN BAY - LINGSHAN ISLAND:

An exciting PANORAMIC of the island.
A Helicopter swoops before us. Sweeping over
the central mountains, valleys and lush tree
forests of Lingshan.
About Nine-Hundred-Meters inland from its
far Eastern Bay, the 'X' point is marked by a
laser and GPS from the Helicopter cockpit.

Colonel Longwei reminisces a past image. . .

"When I was here in '71 for PLA Special Forces
Maneuvers, the locals talked vaguely about a
time, when many large boats brought new
people into the mountains, at the edge of this
Bay."

Longwei is mic'd-up with an aviation headset
in the right seat across from the H-Pilot.
Shoulder bandaged. He turns to face Bohai
and Meifeng, in the cabin's rear seats.

"At the time, I thought it was a mistranslation.
They have a different 'dialect' out here. They
talked of evil 'Red Dragon' Soldiers. And spoke
about the 'Kree. .sees Slave' people.

Bohai suggests a thought. . .

"'Kree. .sees', that's got to be the captured
Koreans. . ."

He presses his face against the glass.

"They were the other 'Slave Labor' Japan brought in to build the Tunnels, the Forge and eventually the 'Gold Bullion' Vaults."

Pauses watching the passing countryside.

"I've kite-surfed this place many times, but never considered this possibility . . ."

Meifeng quietly includes her view. . .

"The 'Japanese Supply Destroyers' must have used this Bay to off-load the looted 'Gold from Qingdao', as well!"

Longwei jumps back in . . .

"Up ahead. . . Look!"

Below, the pagoda trees and thick forest, thin-out, into a 'Valley Entrance'.
They all spot a 'nick' in the landscape, a 'Hill', where only scrub trees and bushes are growing. It's different. It's land that's receded.

"Bohai, you said you've been here?"

"Yeah. Just East of that 'Hill', Colonel."

"Bohai. . . that's no 'Hill' . . that's your 'Vault Entrance'!"

It hits Bohai and Meifeng like a 'slab of bricks'. They look. They realize. They triple check their sanity. And now they can visually see it. . .

Stacked - Forged Gold Bullion Bars

THE HILL - LINGSHAN ISLAND:
Everyone is working 'Shovels', as a local
backhoe operator 'Rips" into the harder
ground at the 'Hill Location'.
A trench Ten-Meters deep has been dug out of
the hard earthworks as . . .

THUNK!
Bohai's shovel strikes a 'Metal Door.

Bohai, Meifeng and Longwei all stare at each
other. Excitement twinkles in their eyes.

The high pitched 'CREAKING' sound of ailing
ancient 'Metal', groans, as the Door is opened.

'BLACKNESS' only, as they peer inside. Then
shafts of light spill in from outside, with
dislodged dirt tumbling inward.

Their eyes quickly adjust and view an intricate 'Tunnel Network", running back at least a football field length.

THE LINGSHAN CAVE VAULT:
Bohai enters first.
Followed by Meifeng and Longwei. All of them absolutely stunned.
Flashlights cut the opaque gloom like lasers.
Bohai comments, as he climbs in . . .

"The Interior appears perfectly preserved since 1945. . ."

Bohai halts.
Meifeng follows his LIGHT beam to . . .
Walls stacked with. . .
Unmarked wooden PALLETS.

The Colonel takes his shovel and smashes one . . .as. . .
CRACK.
A pallet splits open to reveal rows of Forged 'Gold Bullion Bars'.
Neatly stacked and ordered like soldiers at attention.
Gleaming bright in the half-light.

Shocked, Colonel Longwei catches site of something else. Something HORRIBLE.

A steel gated 'Tunnel', filled with Hundreds of 'Rotted Corpses and Skeletons' wedged up to the 'Steel Fence Gate', in an attempt to claw their way out.

Meifeng walks up ahead of her Uncle. . .

"The 'Horror', it must have been for all these People! They all suffered so much and died for what?"

And suddenly, their happy moment, is met with an 'austere silence'. . .

A moment, only broken when Bohai says. . .

"You're right, Mei. This 'Gold' doesn't belong to us."

Their taciturnity reveals, they all AGREE.

Then, Meifeng's mind suddenly ignites. . .

"Being a 'Good Guy' is one thing, but being a 'Treasure Hunter' makes me sure. . . Sovereign Treasure can ALWAYS be taken back by its 'Original Owners'. . .So. . ."

Bohai answers for her. . .

"You've got to keep an 'Eye Out' for who's offering the biggest 'Finder's Fee'. . ."

"RIGHT. . . Babe!"

"And, Mei, our own PRC, has had a 'Big Ten-Percent Finder's Fee' on 'ALL' Found 'JAPANESE LOOTED GOLD & TREASURE', since 1946!"

The weight of all of this new knowledge about the 'Treasure find' is both sad and exciting. . .

Then, Meifeng gets a twinkle in her eye. . .

"Ultimately, this "Finder's Fee', means we'll
have 'Huntin' Money' to go after even more
'Treasure' finds all over Asia!

We're gonna OWN that 'Dragon' superyacht
Jiang's been playing with and. . .
We're going on a new 'Dragon Gold Quest'!"

"You and me, Mei?"

"Yes, You and Me, Babe, together Again!"

Thinking about that. A 'wry smile', on Bohai.
And a 'glint of pure adventure', on Meifeng!

And you just know, they're going to go for a
life together as. . .

Superyacht 'The Dragon'

. . . Bohai and Meifeng 'kite fly' over, with their
'CHINESE DRAGONS' displayed, on each of
their kites. . .

. . .While below them, The 'Superyacht Dragon' sails silently into the 'calm' Seas of a 'Tropical Pacific Island'. . .and Hang adds his own final tribute. . .

"At Long Last, "Bohai the Kite-Surfer' can now truly become. . . 'The Boy Who Rode The Dragon'. . . "

Relaxing together, Colonel Longwei, XO Hang and Captain Jiang, puff on newly lit Cubans Cigars, as they sit back on 'The Dragon's' upper deck chairs, drinking expensive Scotch Whisky, and smiling at Bohai and Meifeng as the two 'Lovers' kite-sail into the Sunset. . .

AN INTERNATIONAL NEWS SERVICE BROADCAST:
Playing on ALL the Superyacht's Satellite Televisions, a news service Broadcaster appears on screen. . .

He's blown away by what he's about to read. . .

". . . And in International News.
An anonymous Group has repatriated 'Fifty-Seven-point-Seven-Billion US Dollars' in 'Gold Bullion', to the 'Peoples Republic of China'. . .

It is believed that the 'GOLD BULLION BARS' were looted from 'China' during WWII by 'Japanese Occupation Forces'.

The Gold was sequestered on Island Hideaways within underground 'Storage Vaults' since 1944.
These Islands are scattered throughout 'The Yellow Sea', off the coast of Northern China.

Images appear in the background, showing scenes from several islands, with 'Gold Bullion' in the underground vaults. . .

"In addition, China will redistribute portions of these 'GOLD BULLION' funds amongst all of their Provinces based on 'Populations' with an emphasis on those people 'Directly Affected by the Horrors of WWII'. . .

This is the 'Biggest Find' of 'GOLD BULLION' in Modern History. . ."

THE END